PHOTOGRAPHY
Walter Michot, Joe Rimkus Jr.,
David Bergman, C.M. Guerrero

With contributions by:
Al Diaz, Chuck Fadely,
Carl Juste, Bill Frakes,
A. Enrique Valentin,
A. Brennan Innerarity
and
Beth A. Keiser

ON THE COVER
Center fielder Chuck Carr shows why Manager Rene Lachemann says, 'He's the best who has played for me.'

WALTER MICHOT

About the cover photograph:
The wall above the baseball was darkened.

PREVIOUS PAGE
Carr glides along the basepaths, cruising along to a National League-leading 58 stolen bases in 1993.

WALTER MICHOT

NEXT PAGE
Lee Marks of Coconut Grove carries Hunter Marks, 2, along with souvenirs and baby bottle on opening day.

AL DIAZ

MARLINS!
Top of the First

The Miami Herald
The Miami Herald Publishing Company
A Division of Knight-Ridder Inc.

Andrews and McMeel
A Universal Press Syndicate Company
Kansas City

MARLINS!

AUTHOR
Dan Le Batard

BOOK DESIGN
Steve Rice

BOOK EDITOR
Hal Habib

BOOK MANAGER
Elizabeth Grudzinski

PICTURE EDITOR
Katharine P. Smith

THE MIAMI HERALD

PUBLISHER
David Lawrence Jr.

PRESIDENT
Roberto Suarez

GENERAL MANAGER
Joe Natoli

EXECUTIVE EDITOR
Douglas C. Clifton

MANAGING EDITOR
Saundra Keyes

**DIRECTOR OF NEW
BUSINESS DEVELOPMENT**
Barrie Atkin

**ASSISTANT MANAGING
EDITOR / GRAPHICS**
Steve Rice

EXECUTIVE SPORTS EDITOR
Paul Anger

**DIRECTOR OF EDITORIAL ART
AND DESIGN**
Randy Stano

DIRECTOR OF PHOTOGRAPHY
Dennis Copeland

COLOR PRINTING
Michael R. Springer
Ramon DeJesus

Marlins! Top of the First
copyright © 1993 by The Miami Herald
Publishing Company, a division of Knight-
Ridder. All rights reserved. Printed in the
United States of America. No part of this
book may be used or reproduced in any
manner whatsoever without written permis-
sion except in the case of reprints in the
context of reviews. For information, write
Andrews and McMeel, a Universal Press
Syndicate Company, 4900 Main Street,
Kansas City, Missouri 64112.

Library of Congress Catalog Card Number:
93-74100

ISBN: 0-8362-8054-7

CONTENTS

FIRST PITCH
A crowd of 42,334 basks in the sunshine during the 6-3 opening-day victory over the Dodgers.
CHUCK FADELY

BIG LEAGUE!

South Florida grows up: Just look at us now!

By Edwin Pope
Herald Sports Editor

I came to The Miami Herald, as I recall, Sept. 11, 1956 — without the faintest illusion that South Florida would ever get big-league baseball. My only reasons for coming were, first, I believed The Herald had the best sports section in America, and, second, I had quit another job in a bit of a snit when that management refused to underwrite a $1.75 pencil sharpener.

We used pencils then. We weren't even up to electric typewriters, let alone computers. Dark Ages across the board.

It would be 10 more years before Miami acquired the Dolphins, nearly a quarter-century before pro basketball arrived, nearly four decades to ice hockey in South Florida. No one was so rosy-eyed a fool as to dream of big-league baseball before the turn of the century.

But, baby, look at us now!

No more "bush!"

I first heard the expression from Chicago Tribune columnist Dave Condon, who was incapable of mentioning South Florida without describing it as bush-league. "Some century, if you're lucky," Condon would say, "you might get pro football and basketball. But you'll *never* get baseball."

Oh? Then what were those 3,064,847 fans doing around Joe Robbie Stadium in the summer of 1993? How was it that only 21 other baseball teams ever drew more?

I later heard the "bush!" slur on South Florida sports from radio-TV's Hank Goldberg. Notice how less often Our Henry used the word as the season went on and the fans kept coming?

South Florida is not now, and never was, bush. South Floridians have always been choosy about how they spend their time and money because they have so many alternatives. Like beaches and sailing and fishing waters, like tennis courts and golf courses, like horse racing and jai-alai and greyhound racing.

The true revelation of the Marlins was that so many people came to see an inferior team. Not inferior by expansion standards, for it had the fifth-best record of a dozen expansion teams, but inferior by competitive standards.

They couldn't hit. They weren't always too hot at fielding, either. So many balls disappeared in right field it became a regular Black Hole. They pitched pretty good awhile, but not in the second half.

The last words I heard from a 1993 Marlin summed it up. The finale, a 9-2 loss to the Mets, had been called after eight-plus innings. When it ended, Orestes Destrade, my favorite Marlin, was on first base after singling through a minor monsoon.

"I'm up there against Mike Maddux looking for a windshield wiper and a fastball and all I'm getting is rain and breaking stuff," Destrade said. "He finally threw me a fastball, and I hit it, but that's the way it's been all year — a real struggle."

Always will be. That's why we go. But when baseball landed and gave me another reason to love this end of the peninsula, we also killed the "bush!"

May it *never* grow back.

WE DID IT
Owner Wayne Huizenga hugs Manager Rene Lachemann on closing day. Overhead, a plane flew by with a banner: 'We did it! Over three million fans. Thank you, Wayne & the Marlins.'

CARL

Carl Barger lived — and died — for the Marlins

Back before the Marlins became something that could be embraced, Carl Barger walked into an office that was empty enough to echo. He was on the third floor of a Fort Lauderdale office building in August of 1991, sun shining strong through the windows. The atmosphere was otherwise antiseptic, like a hospital delivery room before birth.

Barger's phone rang. He was a powerful executive, a lawyer who made himself a millionaire, but he didn't have anyone to answer his calls yet. He was, for the moment, the sole employee of South Florida's major-league baseball team. Never mind a receptionist; Barger didn't even have a desk.

The president of the Marlins stepped over the weaving wires, bent down in his suit and answered the phone on his floor.

"Everywhere I've been, you could get things done by just pressing a button," he said. "We are going to have to start here by building the damn button."

That's how it began.

Back before Charlie Hough and Chuck Carr and Benito Santiago gave this team personality, the president of the Marlins was alone on the third floor, building the button. South Florida's team was tucked between a bank and an accounting firm in this big building, identified as "Florida Marlins Inc." in cold letters on the elevator directory.

Barger's job was to turn this team

DENNIS COPELAND

TRIBUTE
The Marlins' uniforms honor their late president, Carl Barger.

into something warm.

The task, much like parenthood, was rough but rewarding. The Marlins grew up quickly. One day the team was all about computers and cabinets and cash and then suddenly South Florida's own players were walking onto a field that had no footprints. In between, the Marlins had to spend $12,000 on practice baseballs (because they didn't have any) and had to shoo away cows from their practice facility (because they had too many).

Carl Barger, as it turned out, died for the Marlins. The 16-hour days sapped all the strength from a man who seemed to have a surplus. Barger ignored the warnings. He lost 25 pounds, fell down dizzy one day while at the home of friend Jim

Leyland, the manager of the Pittsburgh Pirates.

Barger spent that night at the hospital, and promised to slow down, but friends swear they saw him making work-related phone calls right there from his hospital bed.

Less than a month later, Barger was moving too fast again. He was the speaker at an informal dinner for a group of truckers, and awkwardly out-dressed everyone by wearing one of his four tuxedos. He had to. He had another speaking engagement one hour later, at a formal dinner. There wasn't enough time to change, his attire or his attitude.

In December of 1992, at the age of 61, Barger collapsed in the lobby of the Louisville, Ky., hotel where baseball was holding its annual meetings. This time he didn't get up. He lived long enough to acquire the team's players. He didn't live long enough to see them play. At Barger's funeral, in memory of the man who said he knew batting averages before he knew the alphabet, the organist played *Take Me Out To The Ballgame.*

Four months after Barger's death, the Marlins won the very first game they played, 6-3, over the Los Angeles Dodgers. Marlins owner H. Wayne Huizenga looked up toward the postcard-blue sky that afternoon of April 5 and, tears streaming down his cheeks, thanked Barger for sending South Florida a slice of heaven.

PUT YOUR LEFT ARM IN . . .

No, they never told Wayne Huizenga that owning a baseball team would be so glamorous. But during a break in the action against the Pirates, Billy has him dancing the hokeypokey. A curtain call was hoped for on closing day. 'Not in a million years,' he said.

WAYNE

Wow, what a difference: Business becomes pleasure

This was in July of 1991, a couple days after he had written the check for $95 million. Marlins owner H. Wayne Huizenga sat in a spacious boardroom, hands folded on a brown oak table in the center of his empire. He was explaining why he had bought into baseball.

Huizenga had made much of his $670 million here, at the headquarters of Blockbuster Entertainment in Fort Lauderdale, but not a cent had been earned because he was a romantic. No, no, no, Huizenga said, he didn't buy the Marlins to fix the emptiness his hometown felt every time the boys of summer went to play somewhere else at the end of the spring.

Huizenga was a third baseman at Pine Crest high school in Fort Lauderdale, but that was a long time ago. He wasn't the type to indulge in baseball poetry about green fields and sunshine and pitches thrown perfectly. When Huizenga was asked why he had purchased a baseball team, he gave an icy answer that had nothing to do with a father watching a game with his boy.

"This," he said, "is a diversification of my portfolio."

Huizenga drove a garbage truck at 22 and within a decade turned his small, smelly business into the world's largest waste-management corporation. He went from garbage man to entertainment tycoon, went from owning a group of garbage trucks to owning a yacht, three jets and a collection of classic cars. So, yes, Huizenga, 55, is an impressive business man, but he is something else, too:

He is the reason South Florida got major-league baseball.

Denver and St. Petersburg had long been considered heavy favorites to get 1993's two expansion teams — they had been clamoring for years — but South Florida jumped to the forefront the moment Huizenga said he wanted in. Baseball's owners wanted one wealthy man, not a team of investors like St. Petersburg offered. They didn't mind that Huizenga had once referred to a fly ball as a "transaction."

In fact, if Huizenga had lived 300 miles northwest, if he had lobbied for a team in St. Petersburg instead of South Florida, Joe Robbie Stadium would have been empty throughout the summer of 1993.

As it was, South Florida got its team and Huizenga immediately hired Pittsburgh Pirates President Carl Barger, a close friend who sold Huizenga on baseball's charms whenever the two would fly to the Dominican Republic for one of their weekend golf binges. Barger hired General Manager Dave Dombrowski from Montreal, and Dombrowski, in turn, hired some of the best scouts in baseball — luring them with Huizenga's pile of money.

'Overall, as Dick Clark would say, I give it an 86. Very danceable. But I don't think he should leave his day job.'

ORESTES DESTRADE,
First baseman and noted dance critic, after seeing team owner H. Wayne Huizenga do the hokeypokey

And so it was that on Nov. 17, 1992, the day the Marlins selected 36 players from other teams in the major-league expansion draft, Huizenga stood in a New York hotel lobby — still business before baseball. A day earlier, he had completed a $185 million purchase of Sound Warehouse. A day later, he needed to be in Europe in the morning to buy something else.

His jet was waiting for him at the airport, ready to leave as soon as he got this baseball thing out of the way.

Behind Huizenga, on a billboard, were the names of all the players

11

the Marlins had selected. A reporter asked Huizenga if the Marlins intended to keep Bryan Harvey, one of the new Marlins on the board. Huizenga shrugged and then admitted that he had no idea who Harvey was. Nonetheless, he would be paying this Harvey guy $11 million over the next three years.

I t took some work, but the Marlins changed the man. Huizenga attended just about every home game, came over in a helicopter sometimes just so he could be on time. He sometimes cut business meetings short so he could be at the park by the first inning. He came dressed casually, signed autographs and got catsup on his shirt.

By the end of the year, Huizenga was cheering Harvey just like everyone else in Joe Robbie Stadium. More often than not, he would even come to the ballpark with his son.

"I have become a baseball fan," Huizenga said through a smile on the season's last day — one wonderful season having changed a man, and South Florida, forever.

GREAT END TO A GREAT START

Boynton Beach teacher Jim Wade and son Tristan, 8, cheer the final out on opening day.
AL DIAZ

13

OPENING DAY

ELECTRICITY IN THE AIR

Severe thunderstorms rocked JRS and jolted owner Wayne Huizenga awake at 4 a.m. on April 5, opening day. 'Don't worry,' his wife Marti told him. 'It will be fine.' And it was.

PATRICK FARRELL

	1	2	3	4
LA	0	0	0	0
FLA	0	3	1	0

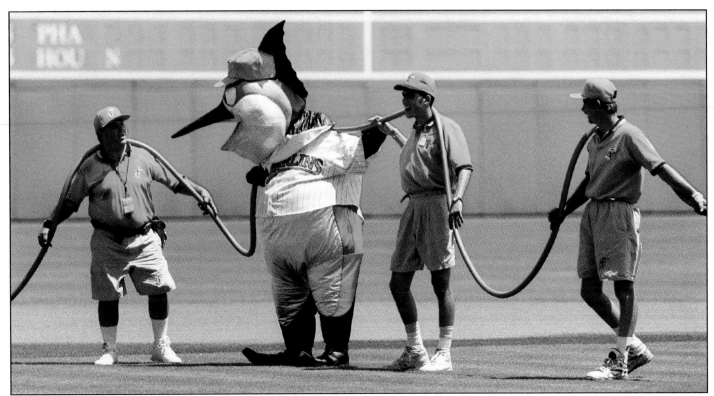

A FISH INTO WATER
Billy The Marlin helps the grounds crew water down the diamond at Joe Robbie Stadium before opening ceremonies.

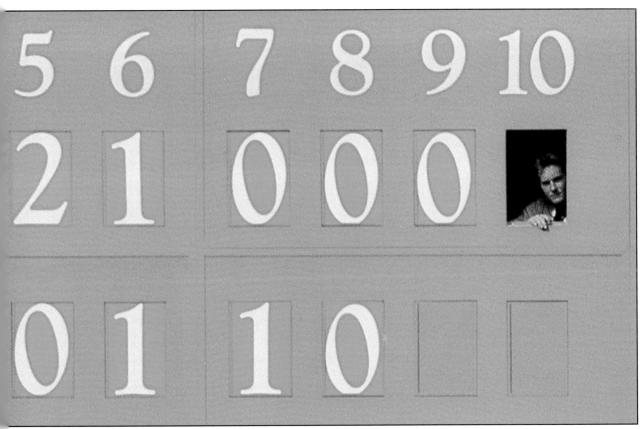

KNOTHOLE VIEW
The converted JRS included a manually operated scoreboard — and numbers that had the crowd cheering.

'It was the first day, and I was walking out to the mound to make the first pitch. That walk doesn't usually carry much emotion for me, but this was something else, something special. The grass, the sunshine, the crowd. Just the feeling. I'll never forget that walk to the mound, not as long as I live.'

CHARLIE HOUGH

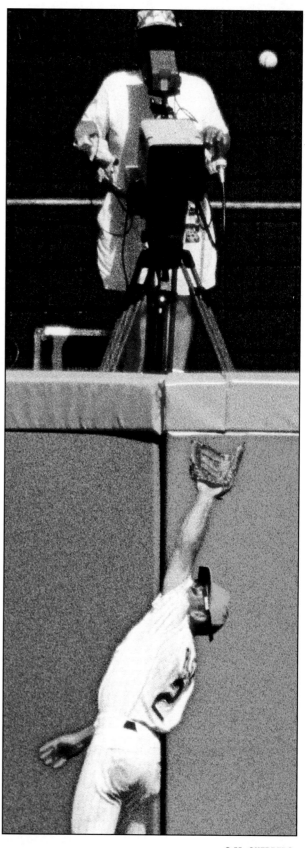

C.M. GUERRERO

A. BRENNAN INNERARITY

FIRST TWO RUNS

Benito Santiago, left, greets Jeff Conine as they both score on Walt Weiss' triple in the second. Catcher Mike Piazza is in the center.

STRIKE A POSE

Scott Pose, on his spectacular catch: 'It was special. Now when I look back, it was — because it's possible I'll never get to make one like that again. It's something nobody can take away.'

FINAL OUT
Benito Santiago and Bryan Harvey closed the door on the Dodgers, 6-3.

PATRICK FARRELL

CHARACTERS

PLEASE, CHUCK!
Chuck Carr tries to oblige as
many autograph-seeking fans as
possible. He signs more
autographs than any Marlin.

BILL FRAKES

& CARICATURES

Do voodoo, rock, philosophy, surfing mix? They yabba-dabba do!

If Marlins center fielder Chuck Carr hadn't been born, Walt Disney would have created him. The cocky Carr, part cartoon and part character, added a flash of fluorescence to a game capable of being as black and white as its box scores. Carr might have stood out like neon on other teams, the way he rolled up his uniform sleeves so fans could enjoy his muscles, but he blended neatly into a Florida clubhouse void of clones or cliches.

The Marlins had a second baseman who surfed and a first baseman who spoke three languages.

They had a pitcher who enjoyed reading complex philosophers and another who liked writing poetry on rainy days.

They had a relief pitcher who bathed in magic liquid his father sent from Puerto Rico and a utility player who blew cigar smoke in the face of the lucky voodoo doll in his locker.

They had a shortstop who named his puppy Springsteen and claimed that playing the drums with John Fogerty was a bigger thrill than playing in the World Series.

They had a farm-boy reliever who earned more than $4 million in 1993 but still was humble enough to pump gas at his father-in-law's convenience store in the winter.

They had a general manager who liked fine wine and Broadway shows and a manager who preferred Budweiser and the Beach Boys.

They had a left fielder who liked to snuggle with sea lions and a 45-year-old pitcher who smoked cigarettes on the exercise bike and a catcher who rode limousines to games and . . .

In short, they had personality.

Start with a colorful Carr that ran like new.

NOW BATTING

Manager Rene Lachemann pencils in Alex Arias as a pinch hitter for Charlie Hough in the sixth inning on opening day. 'It's beautiful to get that first win over with,' Lachemann said. 'It was a very emotional day. The first game in Florida.'

Four teams had given up on Carr before he came to the Marlins, had given up because he had never produced statistics as large as his ego. But Carr excelled with the Marlins, leading the National League in three categories:

1) Stolen bases
2) Great catches
3) Biggest head

Carr once called himself "the best center fielder in the world" and talked about making a personal highlight film titled *Classic Carrs*.

Carr, 25, could back up his talk, though. He led the NL with 58 stolen bases in 1993. He made so many wonderful catches — on balls other center fielders wouldn't have even touched — that Manager Rene Lachemann said he has never had a better center fielder. Carr was so fast he could go from zero to hero in no time flat.

St. Louis Manager Joe Torre said he had never seen a catch as splendid as the one a careening Carr made against his team. On his next trip to St. Louis, Carr made a better one.

Carr won a game in Montreal by bunting home a run in the ninth inning even though Expos Manager Fclipe Alou knew it was coming. Alou had seen Carr do the same thing a week earlier against the Mets.

After the game, Carr gave his interviews while staring into a mirror.

Carr wanted to name his only son Sports — get it? Sports Carr? — but his wife wouldn't allow it. Carr loves all children, signs more autographs than any Marlin. His wife has to call him in for dinner because he is roller skating in the street with the neighborhood kids.

Carr was only one of the most colorful characters on a team filled with them. Even the men who molded the Marlins, General Manager Dave Dombrowski and Manager Rene Lachemann, were extreme opposites.

C.M. GUERRERO

CONINE THE ADVENTURER

Left fielder Jeff Conine has a flair for the spectacular. His off-season plans include being dropped in a cage into a Great White Shark feeding frenzy. He says that will be the 'ultimate. I mean, hitting three home runs in a game off Dave Stewart would be pretty outstanding, too, but Dave Stewart can't kill you.'

In fact, they had little more in common than a want to win.

Dombrowski kept his hair neatly trimmed. He wore impeccable suits whether he was at a banquet or a ballpark. He would have his tie neatly knotted even if he was standing on the surface of the sun.

Lachemann had the long, blond hair of a surfer. He would show up at news conferences wearing shorts and a baseball cap. He would do his postgame interviews in his underwear.

Dombrowski liked fine wine and Broadway shows and, when he got really mad, would actually say things like "Jiminy Cricket." Lachemann

DOINK!

Charlie Hough shows the batting form that caused him to go 13 years without a hit. Hough reports that they no longer make bats with his signature. 'You have to get a hit more than once every 13 years to have an autographed bat,' he says.

liked beer, loud rock 'n' roll and he didn't need to be angry to spew obscenities in every direction.

Dombrowski liked playing squash. Lachemann liked lifting weights.

Dombrowski acquired the Marlins. Lachemann taught them. Together, they put together a team with personalities as different as their own.

Take left fielder Jeff Conine, for example. He is a racquetball champion with a serve clocked at 150 miles per hour. His bat is pretty quick, too. Conine was one of baseball's best rookies in 1993 — he hit .292 — and he is an adventurer, too.

He planned off-season escapades that included an African safari, a hot-air balloon ride and an Australian excursion during which, for $10,000, he will be caged and dumped into a Great White Shark feeding frenzy.

Conine, 27, loves all animals, visits the zoos in various National League cities. When he was playing in the minor leagues in 1992, in Omaha, Neb., he befriended a zoo keeper who let him in after hours to frolic in the big-cat exhibit.

On one day off during the 1993 season, Conine went to Key West and swam with dolphins. Lachemann was on the beach later that day. He saw someone float by overhead, gliding through the air while tied to the back of a moving boat. Lachemann figured out later that the parasailor was his left fielder.

Conine was married in October. The reception was held in an aquarium.

Conine shouldn't invite second baseman Bret Barberie to his new home. Barberie might want to surf in Conine's 300-gallon fish tank. Barberie, 26, is a die-hard dude, a kid who went surfing after spring-training practices and rented an apartment on Hollywood beach so he could surf before games.

If he hadn't been a professional baseball player, Barberie says he would have been a professional

WALTER MICHOT

THE CLOSER

Pittsburgh Manager Jim Leyland, on Bryan Harvey: 'He's brilliant. When the Marlins go into the ninth inning with a lead, they are the best team in the division.'

skateboarder. He owned a station wagon in high school. It was painted with flowers.

When Barberie was at spring training in West Palm Beach in 1989, Hurricane Hugo was kicking up large waves. Barberie was eating in a McDonald's, bumming because he didn't have a surfboard with him, but he improvised. He stole a food tray — the one that had been under his french fries — and used it as a surfboard. He rode the six-foot waves all afternoon.

"It was awesome," he said.

Barberie, a born-again Christian who reads the Bible each evening before sleeping, quit chewing tobacco because he thought kids might get a bad impression of him. Relief pitcher Richie Lewis can't quit. He

BILL FRAKES

SURFIN' USA (AND ELSEWHERE)

Bret Barberie, surfer dude, gives you his favorite spots to catch a cool wave:

5) "Australia, even though I haven't been there. They tell me that you ride a wave and just keep going for 30 minutes. That's one of my dreams right there. It'll probably be No. 1, after I go. They have shark-restraining nets. Problem is they're not reliable."

4) Sebastian Inlet, Fla.: "Those waves surprised me."

3) Salt Creek, Calif.: "The 10-foot waves are the largest I've ever ridden. But the water is only two feet shallow. You fall off a wave that big, and you're talking broken bones."

2) Laguna Beach, Calif.: "The water is as clear as it can be, and the waves are hollow."

1) Rosarito, Mexico: "Secluded beaches. And, of course, the waves are awesome."

SURF'S UP, DUDE

'I'm still in search of the perfect wave,' second baseman Bret Barberie says. 'It is a quest.'

says he hasn't pitched a competitive inning since 1982 without a fist-sized wad of tobacco in his left cheek.

"If I didn't have it," Lewis said, "I'd probably be so lopsided I'd fall right off the mound."

Reliever Bryan Harvey, accent soaked in the South, kept two huge cases of tobacco in his locker, cases large enough to hold small refrigerators. Harvey is a down-home type who married his high school sweetheart in North Carolina and still lives on a 450-acre ranch there. He drives a pickup truck. One of Harvey's favorite things is to get knee deep in mud and chase his cows. He gives them their shots, too.

One cold day in Chicago, Harvey was hobbled so much by a groin pull that he needed help to get down the dugout stairs between innings. Still, in the ninth inning, he struck out all three Cubs he faced. Harvey might have been baseball's best reliever in 1993.

BORN TO ROCK

Shortstop Walt Weiss, who wakes up neighbors playing the drums and has a puppy named Springsteen, gives you his favorite five songs in the world:

5) *Pink Houses*, by John Mellencamp.
4) *Darkness On The Edge Of Town*, by Bruce Springsteen.
3) *Werewolves Of London*, by Warren Zevon.
2) *Tunnel of Love*, by Dire Straits.
1) *Jungleland*, by Springsteen.

SURE-HANDED SHORTSTOP

Shortstop Walt Weiss warned that the Marlins 'should get used to failure,' but was one of the team's major success stories.

DAVID BERGMAN

'They helped me when I was little, so now I help them when I'm big. I would do anything for them. I've always wanted to take them away from the poverty. I owe them. They made me a man.'

BENITO SANTIAGO,
Catcher, who earns
more than $3 million a season,
explaining why he still lives with his
parents at age 28.

JOE RIMKUS JR.

WHY IS THIS MAN LAUGHING?
The Marlins beat the Astros, 5-4, in 13 innings on Aug. 26 in one of their strangest victories of the season. Pitcher Richie Lewis drove in the winning run, pitcher Chris Hammond was sent up as a pinch hitter and catcher Benito Santiago played an inning in left field. 'I'm not a clown out there,' Santiago insisted.

WALTER MICHOT

MY RACING SHADES
Benito Santiago owns a $237,000 Lamborghini Diablo, which includes doors that open by going up. He specializes in getting around in style. He takes limousines from his hotel suite (yes, suite) to the stadium for road games.

29

CRABBY

Orestes Destrade rates Osaka Joe's Stone Crabs in Japan up there with a hanging curve.

WALTER MICHOT

CHARACTERS & CARICATURES

Charlie Hough was Florida's best starting pitcher, startling when you consider that he was old enough to be the father of fellow pitcher David Weathers (23). Hough, 45, was the oldest player in the National League, a man who had a longer tenure in major-league baseball than his boss, Manager Rene Lachemann. When he walked through the team's hotel, Hough often was mistaken for a coach or trainer. Fans cheered when Hough so much as hit a foul ball.

It was amusing the way Hough sat out stretching exercises and was allowed to finish a distant last in running drills. Hough worked hard, don't misunderstand, but he didn't need the same type of training others did. His success was founded in a fluttering, feathery pitch that fooled.

The knuckleball is so mysterious that even its name lies; it isn't thrown with the knuckles at all. Some of the league's best hitters, like Pittsburgh's Andy Van Slyke and Philadelphia's John Kruk, said they would rather face Bryan Harvey's 95 mile-per-hour fastball than the soft magic that floated from Hough's fingertips like soap bubbles in the wind.

"He just beat us and half the peo-

ple in our lineup are young enough to be his son," Los Angeles center fielder Brett Butler said. "That makes him kind of special, doesn't it?"

Hough, who grew up in Hialeah, 20 minutes from Joe Robbie Stadium, was so excited about playing for his hometown team that he didn't even know what he was earning ($800,000 a year) until a week after he already had agreed to a contract.

Hough is comical, making fun of himself and his age. He was hit by a line drive and explained that his foot didn't swell because "it is an old foot."

A reporter who had enjoyed an interview with Hough shook his hand and joked that interviewing him was "like pulling teeth." Hough responded by pulling out his false teeth.

"That wasn't so hard," he said.

Back in spring training, Hough was asked if he is always self-deprecating and responded: "Maybe I would be, if I knew what that meant."

Pitcher Jack Armstrong, 28, knew what that meant. He is a man of substantive vocabulary. Armstrong's problem was that he was often too smart for his own good. With a critical situation before him, bases loaded and two out, Armstrong sometimes would be searching for worldly answers when what he really needed to find was his fastball.

Right there on the mound, Armstrong would think about social problems or religion or whether he was being a selfish father. He read various philosophers, studied various religions, wondered about the relevance of playing a game for a living.

He was an oxymoron, attaching worth to winning even when he knew winning wasn't that important.

FIRST FREEBIE

Chris Morrell of Merritt Island, Fla., catches the first foul ball of spring.

WALTER MICHOT

He was someone who didn't believe pitching had social relevance, but also felt it had to be important simply because he was doing it. After one loss, Armstrong destroyed the clubhouse so viciously that he had scars all over his hands.

"You should get used to failure," Marlins shortstop Walt Weiss said, accent as New York as a steaming manhole. "This is a game of failure."

Weiss is one of the nicest men in baseball. When fans found out Bruce Springsteen was his idol, they sent him more than 200 bootleg Springsteen tapes. Weiss played his first few years in Oakland, developed a strong following there. When he visited nearby San Francisco with the Marlins, he had his own fan club in left field — holding signs and cheering whatever he did in batting practice.

Weiss, 29, was smooth and spectacular, making some of the best plays you'll see from a shortstop. He was, like Springsteen, always wearing jeans and a T-shirt. When he was named rookie of the year in Oakland, he showed up as the worst-dressed guy at the ceremony. GQ Magazine wanted to do a photo shoot of Weiss and Barberie, but Weiss declined because the magazine was too stuffy for his style.

Weiss got a flat tire one day on the way to Shea Stadium in 1993, stopped on the highway and fixed it himself. He got four hits that afternoon in a victory over the Mets.

Catcher Benito Santiago doesn't do flat tires. The Marlins made him a wealthy man — giving him $7.2 million for two seasons, which he enjoyed spending. Among other things, he rented limousines that would take him from the hotel to the stadium for road games.

"I felt like a king," utility infielder Alex Arias said one time after riding with Santiago.

Santiago, 28, was once late to a game in New York. He said he hadn't heard his wake-up call. It was ringing far away, in another room of his hotel suite.

Santiago owned a $237,000 Lamborghini Diablo, a sports car so

fast that the manual said he had to break in the engine by going more than 200 miles per hour for the first 15 minutes. Santiago says you should have seen the look on the faces of the guards protecting his Davie home when he drove up for the first time and his car doors opened by going *up*.

Santiago only drove the Diablo on Sundays.

"Probably," said first baseman Orestes Destrade, "because it is a religious experience."

Despite having the worst season of his career with the Marlins, the four-time All-Star always said he was happy. There was a reason: Santiago grew up so poor in Puerto Rico that he dropped out of school in the 10th grade to make money for his family. He says he was tired of picking tomatoes all day, then going to sleep exhausted and being woken by flies near his face.

Destrade, 31, was Santiago's best friend on the team. He came to the Marlins with larger expectations than any other player. He was raised in Miami, a Cuban who had spent the last four seasons as the home-run champion in Japan. The Japanese were so enamored with him that a television crew followed him around the United States and a reporter wrote a book about him.

Back in Japan, Destrade had a band named after him. He was not impressed with this, said it would have been more impressive if his name had been attached to a bank. Destrade was something of an entertainer overseas, dropping to one knee immediately after hitting a home run and making a motion that looked like a man starting a lawn mower. He was more subdued in America, watching his home runs quietly from the batter's box.

"The mind is clear then," Destrade said. "It takes a second for the world to come crashing back in."

Destrade was booed initially, his hometown fans expecting more power from the man, but a second-half surge gave him a fine first season. He won the fans over. Destrade

had one game against first-place San Francisco in which he hit two home runs and drove in six.

Said Lachemann: "A few weeks ago the fans wanted his scalp. Now they want him to come out for two standing ovations. Amazing what a few home runs will do."

The Marlins had two third basemen in 1993, Dave Magadan for the first half and Gary Sheffield for the second. Magadan was the team leader early, owner of a .292 career batting average, but was traded when the Marlins had a chance to get Sheffield, 24 years old and owner of a bat filled with gunpowder.

The Marlins decided to build around Sheffield, made him baseball's highest-paid third baseman by giving him a four-year, $22.45 million contract. Hough said Sheffield had the quickest bat he had seen since Hank Aaron. Sheffield found the game easy. In 1992, he was among the league leaders in home runs and RBI and also had the league's best batting average. When he arrived with the Marlins, he said he could hit .330 every year, if that's what he wanted to do. But he preferred to pull the ball for power. All but two of his home runs the past two years have been to left field. San Diego's Tony Gwynn, perhaps the game's best authority on hitting, said Sheffield could hit .350 if he wanted to start hitting to right field.

The Marlins had tales to tell on their bench and in their bullpen, too.

FINAL CHEER

Rain-soaked fans give Alex Arias and the Marlins a farewell standing ovation. 'I'm going out right now to my truck to drive straight home to North Carolina,' Bryan Harvey said, 'and I'll remember that sound all the way.'

DAVID BERGMAN

Infielder Alex Arias left a thimble full of wine and a partially smoked cigar next to a lucky troll doll he named Paul. By the end of the year, fans had sent him more than 20 similar dolls and all of them stood on Arias' locker like good soldiers. During a personal losing streak, pitcher Chris Hammond thought about stealing them for luck.

Infielder Rich Renteria's face was shattered by a line drive in 1990, and he had to borrow money from his in-laws so that his kids could have Christmas gifts. His agent worked for free. "I am a working man," Renteria said. He was the last man to make the Marlins, with a grand slam in spring training's final week, and was considered one of baseball's most inspiring stories. "He's got a sprinkle of magic in his bat," Bryan Harvey said after Renteria won his

Paul the troll

A TROLL TALE

Alex Arias has more than 50 troll dolls in his home. These are his favorites:

5) Iris Chacon: Has pink hair and is named after a Puerto Rican singer.
4) Marlin The Marlin: Has orange hair, a Marlins uniform and a bat.
3) Junior: Has blue hair and a rock 'n' roll guitar. He was a gift from former right fielder Junior Felix.
2) Joshua: Is the biggest troll, and therefore can beat up all the other trolls except for . . .
1) Paul: He was the orange-haired first doll, and Arias still rubs his hair for lucky hits.

fourth game with a pinch hit.

Reliever Luis Aquino sometimes bathed in magic liquid for luck. Aquino's father was a Santeria priest who sacrificed animals in the name of his god. Luis didn't believe in the religion, but he nonetheless accepted his father's presents, which included the liquid. There had to be a sprinkle of magic in that, too: Aquino's dad, after all, was walking after doctors told him he was paralyzed for life.

Outfielder Henry Cotto said he developed the quickness that helped him steal bases by chasing chickens as a teenager.

Outfielder Matias Carrillo was a former farmer who slept outside and bathed in Mexican canals.

Reliever Matt Turner liked to collect antiques and had a Yosemite Sam tattoo on his shoulder.

Reliever Bob McClure liked to wear leather and owned a collection of motorcycles.

Reliever Richie Lewis, at 5-6 one of the smallest pitchers in major-league history, inspired children with his belief that size shouldn't inhibit.

Pitcher Ryan Bowen liked to write poetry on rainy days.

Reliever Joe Klink, born and raised less than 10 minutes from Joe Robbie Stadium, inhaled cigarettes as if they were a source of oxygen.

Catcher Bob Natal looked so much like Fred Flintstone that he kept Fred's baseball card on his locker.

Right fielder Junior Felix enjoyed watching cartoons more than anything and played fly balls as if they were porcupines.

His replacement, rookie Darrell Whitmore, tore up the minor leagues but then saw his swing go silent in the majors.

Pitcher Chris Hammond had perhaps the strangest season of any Marlin, winning eight games in a row at one point and then failing to win even one for the season's next two months.

They were a curious mix, Florida's Marlins, but they made a community stand up and cheer.

MAGIC

From start to finish, the Marlins held us in their spell

It was sunny the afternoon of Feb. 19, 1993, the rain having come a day earlier to wash away baseball's winter worth of gray. The Marlins were, like the weather, new and fresh, and their first day made you feel warm.

Richie Lewis reported to his new team carrying a duffel bag that belonged to the Baltimore Orioles, his former team. Bryan Harvey entered with a jacket that belonged to the California Angels, his former team. Several other players did the same because this tiny team lacked both the little and the large: How could they be expected to have their own equipment when they still didn't even own an identity?

General Manager Dave Dombrowski, the man who had assembled all these new players, went around the locker room introducing himself to players he recognized only by statistics. The players didn't opt for name tags, as had the expansion Colorado Rockies, but they were strangers who would soon become one.

"This feels like the first day of kindergarten," reliever Trevor Hoffman said, "only my mom didn't drop me off this time."

They grew close over time, so close it hurt. Dave Magadan was traded away from his new friends and said he has never missed anything so much in his life. Hoffman

DENNIS COPELAND

MEMORIES
A fan's proud memento autographed by the No. 1 Marlin.

was traded and said that baseball had never left him so depressed. Cris Carpenter, also traded, left quietly and, one week later, in the middle of a pennant race with a winning team in Texas, he sat in a restaurant with his wife and they both cried.

"I was part of something special," Carpenter said the day he left.

The Marlins made magic, created an enthusiasm not normally associated with teams that lose. They lost seven straight games on the road in July — their longest losing streak of the year — and limped home to the comforting embrace of record-break-

ing crowds. In September, 30 games out of first place, the Marlins drew their three millionth fan — giving them more than winning teams from New York to San Francisco.

Charlie Hough has played 24 years. But the old man looked back at the end of Florida's first season, and couldn't help but clutch a moment so crisp and clean it gave him chills.

"It was the first day, and I was walking out to the mound to make the first pitch," Hough said. "That walk doesn't usually carry much emotion for me, but this was something else, something special. The grass, the sunshine, the crowd. Just the feeling. I'll never forget that walk to the mound, not as long as I live."

The Marlins were perfect that first day, winning in the sunshine, months of anticipation finally culminating in the joy of birth. The team was rather imperfect the rest of the way, finishing 64-98 and never winning more than four games in a row, but the fun was in watching them grow.

Floridians had waited so long. They had been teased for years by spring training, the Yankees and Orioles and Braves stopping in like tourists for six weeks of sun and sand. The Marlins weren't visiting, though. They were here for good, and they were welcomed like an old friend.

DAVID BERGMAN

FISHNAPPED

Milt Thompson of the Phillies nabs Billy, who has filed mascot abuse charges with the commissioner.

EASY NOW, CHARLIE

A rare sight: Charlie Hough participates in stretching exercises, loosening up his 45-year-old muscles.

SPRING

The Marlins had 43 days to become a team. It was a stretch.

True stories from spring training:

Pitcher Charlie Hough, 45, reports to take the team physical. He comes out of the trainer's room smoking a cigarette. "They told me I was in decent shape," Hough announces, "if I was 50."

Manager Rene Lachemann looks over his roster and learns the following:

(1) One of his shortstops, Alex Arias, once made five errors on four consecutive ground balls.

(2) His No. 1 pick in the expansion draft, outfielder Nigel Wilson, recently swung at four underhand tosses and missed them all.

(3) His starting center fielder, Chuck Carr, didn't think he could make a catch unless he superstitiously tapped his glove before the ball came down.

Shortstop Walt Weiss is stopped after hitting the first batting-practice pitch. He is asked to sign it. He is told Marlins owner H. Wayne Huizenga wants it. Weiss is asked what will happen when he turns his first double play. "A parade?" Weiss wonders.

Hough throws his first knuckle-ball. Radio announcer Joe Angel describes the pitch as "high and low."

Junior Felix hears a noise while playing right field in an intrasquad game. It sounds like booing. Felix turns around to notice that right behind him, just beyond the fence, there is a herd of cows.

Melbourne radio station WLRQ announces it will award exhibition-game tickets to callers who can answer Marlins' trivia questions. One problem with the contest: The Marlins have no history.

Carr freezes between second and third on a triple. "I didn't pick up Cocoa," Carr says, referring to his third-base coach. Except that his third-base coach is named Cookie (Rojas), not Cocoa. The game is being played in Cocoa.

The Marlins win their first three spring games and promise not to be as bad as the original expansion Mets. The 1962 Mets went 40-120 and were 9½ games out of first place after playing nine games.

The Marlins share a hotel in Homestead with a convention of bagpipers. Many players are awakened late Saturday night by the noise. Says Conine: "Gosh, I just

A parachutist misses the stadium. A convention of bagpipers wakes the Marlins. A reliever bakes gloves. Then things really got weird.

wanted to throw on a kilt and parade around the hotel lobby. But I withheld the urge."

A prankster begins pasting local newspaper headlines on Hough's locker:

HOUGH GUILTY
IN STABBING

HOUGH'S ATTORNEY
QUITS CASE

HOUGH SEEKS TRIAL

"I don't know who has been doing this," an angry Hough says, "but when I find the guy, I'm going to stab him."

Showers and toilets in the Marlins' clubhouse in Homestead overflow, forcing Lachemann to walk across the field with a towel and shower equipment so he can clean up in Cleveland's clubhouse.

Carr has a different solution. "I took a shower in the sink," says Carr, who stands 5-10. "I'm small, so I can do that. It was either the sink or the water fountain."

Lachemann gets back to his hotel room late one Saturday night and, as usual, begins returning phone calls to radio stations that have requested interviews. One particularly interesting interview lasts 10 minutes. It ends with these words from the interviewer: "Thanks a lot, sir. I hope I get a good grade on this."

Pitcher Luis Aquino admits that his love for Mexican food is so strong that he once missed five exhibition games because of it. Aquino burned his pitching hand on a sizzling plate of fajitas and, two springs later, still has the scar. "I still eat Mexican food," he says. "I just stay away from the plates."

WALTER MICHOT

WISE GUY, EH?
A prankster taped these headlines on Charlie Hough's locker. 'When I find the guy,' Hough growled, 'I'm going to stab him.'

Utility infielder Gary Scott gets traded to the Reds for pitcher Chris Hammond. Between trades and demotions, Scott has lived in eight different apartments over the last year. "When I'm done playing, I'm going to start my own moving business," Scott says. "I'm serious."

First baseman Orestes Destrade, fluent in three languages, does infield chatter in Japanese.

Infielder Rich Renteria is invited to practice with the major-leaguers. This is his big chance. But he can't afford a car. So he comes to the park early with the minor-leaguers and sleeps in a locker until the big-league players arrive three hours later.

A 2½ hour bus trip takes more than four hours. First, one of the two buses blows a tire. Then the lead bus goes back to see why the first bus stopped. But the injured bus pulls off at an exit. The lead bus doesn't see this and drives past, all the way back to the starting point. The walkie-talkies aren't working. "Growing pains," says Destrade.

Carr approaches Hall of Famer Lou Brock, a Montreal Expos coach, and asks for tips on how to be a better base stealer. "Listen,

son," Brock tells Carr. "What I've done can't be taught in 15 minutes." Carr settles for an autograph.

The double-play combination of Weiss and second baseman Bret Barberie is supposed to do a modeling shoot for GQ, but the deal falls through. "GQ must have noticed their faces," Destrade says.

A group of local bikers finds out reliever Bob McClure likes to wear leather and owns a collection of 13 Harley-Davidsons. They send him a six-pack of Harley-Davidson beer. It sits untouched in McClure's locker for weeks. "We're afraid to try it," McClure reveals.

Pitcher Jose Martinez misses a scheduled start because he has injured himself with a Q-tip.

Barberie explains that he isn't good at any sport except baseball. He says he can't make a layup when standing all alone on a basketball court. Says third baseman Dave Magadan from a nearby locker: "Bret is the only guy I know who can make billiards a contact sport."

WARMING UP
Center fielder Chuck Carr, left, and Nigel Wilson stretch via the buddy system.

JOE RIMKUS JR.

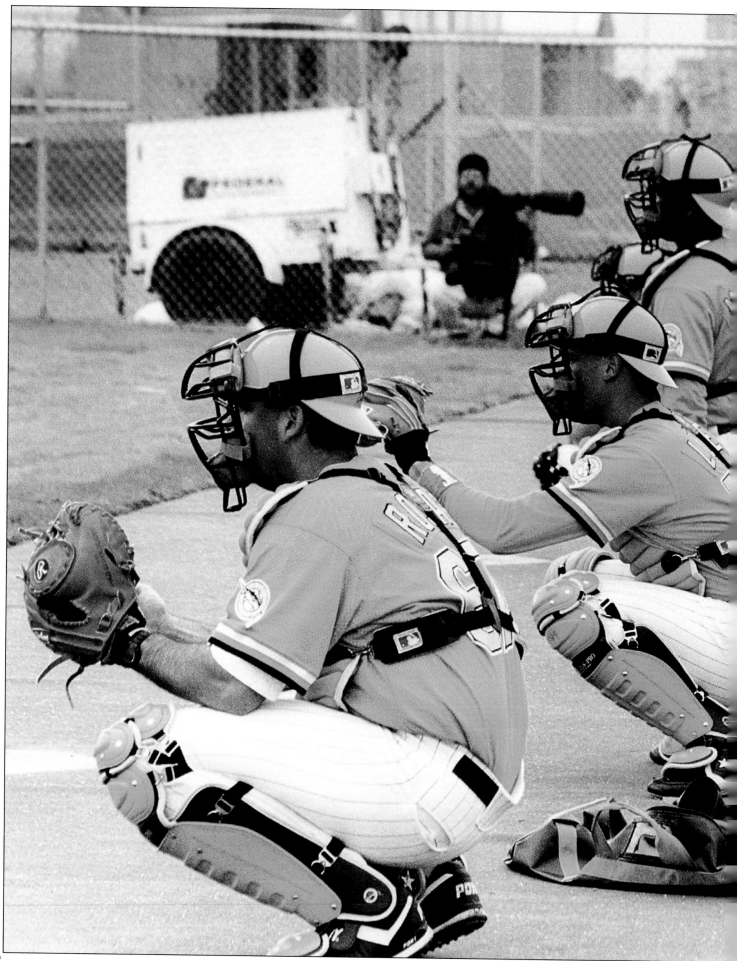

Pitcher Trevor Hoffman reveals his father once sang the national anthem at a major-league game when "the person who was supposed to sing got into a car accident or something." Hoffman recalls being very scared. "I thought my dad would forget the words," Hoffman says. "Here he'd be, in front of 60,000 people, letting down the whole country."

Carr reveals he has to catch the ball one-handed. He once tried to break the habit. The result, he says, was three errors in one game.

Wilson's allergies are so bad he has to keep an asthma inhaler in the back of his uniform pocket. He slides on the inhaler and breaks it.

Reliever Matt Turner takes home the gloves of teammates because he has a secret recipe for making them softer. He applies a little water, a sprinkle of baby oil and a dash of Vaseline. Then he throws the gloves in the dryer and lets them simmer for about one minute. "It can't be too much longer," chef Turner explains, "because then the strings dry up and crack."

Arias, who aspires to be the team's starting shortstop, reveals he once made five errors in a Double A game. It took him only two innings — and it happened on the first four balls hit to him. He bobbled the first, then threw it away for two errors. He missed the next three. "I caught the next one, but it almost went through my legs, too," Arias says. "The crowd gave me a standing ovation."

HOW IT BEGAN

The Marlins get a jump on spring training in Melbourne, Fla. Nearly all players arrived early, although one admitted, 'I'm here early because it was cold at home.'

JOE RIMKUS JR.

43

AL DIAZ

EMOTIONAL HEALING

Billy leads the crowd in cheers as the Marlins beat the Indians twice in exhibitions in Homestead, which had been devasted by Hurricane Andrew six months earlier. 'The guys on the bus know what happened here is a tragedy, but they can't be expected to relate to it the way I can,' first baseman Orestes Destrade said. 'I mean, I played here in high school. I played in South Dade. To see it this way is so sad.'

SPRING

Players arrive at their lockers to find a free gift — a funky-fresh pair of running sneakers. "I feel so fast," Hough says after donning the ugly things, made partly of blue suede and featuring the team logo on the side. "They are," says pitcher Scott Chiamparino, "very sexy."

Outfielder Jeff Conine receives a letter from an 8-year-old boy requesting an autograph. The kid puts $1 in the envelope and explains it is his allowance for the week. "Isn't that sad?" Conine says. "He wrote that he hoped $1 would be enough to cover it." Conine sends the kid his autograph and returns the dollar.

Hoffman, a Single A shortstop as recently as 1991, explains why his pitching arm is so lively. "I am brand new, dude."

The Marlins endure some tense

moments during a game in Sarasota. While they are playing, the Tampa Suncoast Dome — which would have been home for an expansion team except that South Florida got the Marlins instead — proudly stages a garage sale and flea market. "Aw, they don't hate us," Magadan says. "Just a couple of people threw batteries at us — car batteries."

The Marlins play in Plant City, 15 minutes outside the flammable St. Pete-Tampa area. Among the signs greeting them:

MY TWO FAVORITE TEAMS ARE THE PIRATES AND ANYONE WHO BEATS THE MARLINS.

HUIZENGA — GESUNDHEIT!

I GOT YOUR EXPANSION RIGHT HERE, BUD!

Several Japanese reporters come to spring training, following Destrade around. This leads to several interesting conversations.

Marlins player: "How long are you here for?"
Japanese reporter: "Japan."

Pitcher Ryan Bowen gets shelled in the final exhibition game in Jacksonville. "You know what?" Barberie says just before the team boards a flight to South Florida. "This season is going to be fun."

Forty-three days old, and it already has been.

SUMMER

A season's worth of scenes we'll never forget

*What follows in these pages
is a countdown
to the Top of the First –
the funniest, tackiest,
greatest moments of all*

FAST START
Jeff Conine, sliding, hit .292 with 12 homers and 79 RBI and was one of the NL's top rookies in '93.
WALTER MICHOT

HOT BAT

AL DIAZ

Utility infielder Rich Renteria, 32, came out of nowhere to become one of baseball's best bench players. Reliever Bryan Harvey said, 'Late in the game, with a chance to win, you want him up there. It seems like he has a sprinkle of magic in his bat.'

Top 5 Enchanting Stories

5 Pitcher Pat Rapp gets his first big-league victory, says afterward that he hasn't been as good a father and husband as he'd like to be. Rapp has spent the past three off-seasons working construction, 12 hours a day, trying to make the money that will get his wife and 1-year-old son out of the cramped trailer they've lived in while he pursued big-league dreams. Rapp's major-league paycheck (about $75,000) will get the family out of debt. They already have moved into an apartment. "I'm not working in construction this year," he says. "I'm going to be home, like a good father should be."

4 After spending 10 years in the minor leagues, catcher Mitch Lyden finally gets to the majors with the Marlins. Lyden, 28, is a Fort Lauderdale native, but he doesn't get into a game while the Marlins are at home. He gets his first start in Chicago, where his family has flown to see him. With his first major-league swing, Lyden hits a home run over the left-field fence in Wrigley Field. Florida's players say it is the longest ball a Marlin has ever hit, although there was no official length estimate. "It's tough to measure something that lands three blocks away," shortstop Walt Weiss says. First baseman Orestes Destrade is in the bathroom when he hears a loud crack. He comes into the dugout, still pulling up his pants, to see Lyden floating over bases the color of clouds.

3 Utility infielder Rich Renteria is playing with the minor leaguers throughout spring training, wearing a jersey that doesn't even have his name on the back. He plays with the big-league Marlins only when they need extra bodies but hits a grand slam in the 10th inning to win an exhibition against the Expos and, suddenly, he is a Marlin. Renteria, 32, stays with the team all year, showing enthusiasm Dave Magadan says he has never seen from a major-leaguer. Renteria becomes one of baseball's finest bench players and erases a large financial debt. "They should make a movie about him," Marlins Manager Rene Lachemann says. "I'd pay to see it."

2 Center fielder Chuck Carr and his wife Candace experience the joy of raising a child. Candace has been pregnant eight times, but Sheldon, born on Oct. 21, 1992, is the first baby to survive. "We've been through hell a couple of times over," says Candace. Sheldon goes to all of daddy's games, points to papa whenever he sees him on the television screen in the nursery. Chuck won't allow a barber to give Sheldon a haircut because he doesn't want anyone getting near his son with anything as sharp as scissors. "That's my boy," Chuck says.

1 Reliever Bryan Harvey is given credit for helping more than 200 couples discover that their children have a rare neurological disorder known as Angelman's Syndrome. There are only 600 known cases of the disorder in North America, an estimated third discovered after Harvey made his story public. His 6-year-old daughter Whitney was diagnosed with Angelman's after doctors misdiagnosed her as having cerebral palsy. Says Harvey: "She can't talk, but she's learned to point to the refrigerator if she is hungry. She gets her coat if she wants to go somewhere. She's learned to touch a button on a computer that makes a dog bark. She's special because all she knows how to do is love."

'She's special because all she knows how to do is love.'

Bryan Harvey,
talking about
his daughter Whitney, who has
Angelman's Syndrome

DEVOTED DAD

Reliever Bryan Harvey sets an expansion record with 45 saves. But his most important relief project didn't come on the field.

C.M. GUERRERO

51

Top 5 Exchanges

5 Rookie right fielder Darrell Whitmore fouls off two bunts in one at-bat and Manager Rene Lachemann subsequently takes off the bunt sign. But Whitmore tries to bunt again, explaining he wants to help the team by doing the job he has been assigned. Alas, he misses again, striking out. "I don't want my No. 5 hitter bunting in that situation," Lachemann tells Whitmore. "If I'm your No. 5 hitter," Whitmore replies, "why do you have me bunting in the first place?"

4 After the Marlins beat the Mets in an empty Shea Stadium, Carr comments on the diseased atmosphere. "This place is dead," Carr says. "There is no life." Replies Mets second baseman Jeff Kent: "How can a guy who hasn't even gone to the bathroom in every National League stadium say something bad about ours?"

3 Pitcher Charlie Hough takes his 15-year-old son Aaron on all the summer road trips. After pitching eight elegant innings against St. Louis, Hough is surrounded by reporters. Aaron videotapes the interviews, making his father uneasy. "Hey, kid, go get a Coke," Hough says. "Hey, Dad, go get a complete game," Aaron replies.

2 Carr is called out on a close play at first base in Wrigley Field, after which he taunts umpire Jeff Kellogg by pointing repeatedly at his own eyes. Says Kellogg: "I'll remember this, kid. I'll remember this." Replies Carr: "If you are blinded by the speed, don't make the call."

1 Lachemann is ejected for only the fourth time in his 29-year baseball career after an argument with umpire Harry Wendelstedt. The Marlins go on to lose, 9-7, after Wendelstedt changes an out call in mid-motion — allowing the Braves to score three extra runs. Here's how their on-field conversation went :

Wendelstedt: "If your team wasn't so bad, blowing all those leads, my call wouldn't have mattered."

Lachemann: "I'm going to have to apologize to the National League about not being allowed to draft the 1927 Yankees."

Aaron Hough, 15, was dad Charlie's good-luck charm and personal coach. 'Hey, Dad, go get a complete game,' Aaron once suggested.

ROUGH ON HOUGH

Charlie Hough said, 'I must be a bum. I lost my last game.' So son Aaron replied, 'Dad, you've lost your last ten games.'

BILL FRAKES

TAG-TEAM TANGO (next page)

Marlins first base coach Vada Pinson and Manager Rene Lachemann form a tough double-say combination.

JOE RIMKUS JR.

A SACRIFICE

Rookie right fielder Darrell Whitmore had his ups — and downs — at the plate this season.

WALTER MICHOT

LAST LICKS

Chuck Carr could be a little out of breath, or he could be telling an umpire what he thinks of his call. Carr once told an umpire he missed a call because he was 'blinded by the speed.'

DAVID BERGMAN

2 TOP 5
EXCHANGES

ALL SHOOK UP

Shortstop Walt Weiss, turning the double play, passes on the Elvis imitations. Give him the real Springsteen anytime.

JOE RIMKUS JR.

Top 5 Tackiest Moments

'I didn't know you were going to be so ugly. That's OK. I'm no oil painting myself.'

RENE LACHEMANN,
upon meeting Billy the Marlin

5 An imitation Elvis, who for some reason was wearing a purple cape, sings the national anthem before a Colorado game against the Marlins. Says shortstop Walt Weiss: "You know it's a big gig when Elvis shows up. Either that or you're in a 7-Eleven."

4 Having already beaten the Marlins by rubbing magical snake oil on his right arm, Cincinnati pitcher Jose Rijo beats them again. His secret this time? Before the game, he sacrifices two goats.

3 Before a game against the Marlins, Montreal pitcher Dennis Martinez is awarded a trophy for being an outstanding Nicaraguan. The trophy is presented in an on-field ceremony. The trophy is both taller and wider than Martinez.

2 A caller to Rene Lachemann's radio show asks the manager when the heck backup catcher Mitch Lyden is going to play. The caller is Lyden's stepfather.

1 Chuck Carr wears a leather jacket into the clubhouse. On the back is a painting of himself — shirtless, no less.

Top 5 Embarrassing Moments

CLIMBING THE WALLS

Right fielder Junior Felix watches a Pirates home run. In another game against Pittsburgh, he misplayed three balls.

JOE RIMKUS JR.

5 To combat the heat, the Marlins wear shorts during a pre-game practice. Lachemann wears his socks up to his knees, trying to hide his varicose veins. Charlie Hough, 45 years old, figures his milk-bottle legs should draw fans. And Cincinnati pitcher Tim Belcher says Marlins catcher Benito Santiago has such awful-looking knees that he should "wear two pairs of pants."

4 Marlins right fielder Junior Felix misplays three balls against Pittsburgh. The Marlins lose, 13-7, in what Lachemann calls the worst game of the year. Lachemann refers to right field as "the Bermuda Triangle." All of Felix's plays appear on ESPN, accompanied by background music from *The Beverly Hillbillies*.

3 Playing in Los Angeles, Carr tries to make his patented one-hand catch of an easy fly ball. The ball hits the heel of his glove and drops. Fans laugh. Carr attempts to pay a fine for hotdogging after the game, throwing $200 on Lachemann's desk, but Lachemann refuses the cash.

2 The Marlins lose to Mets pitcher Anthony Young. Before beating the Marlins, Young had lost 27 consecutive games over two seasons — the longest personal losing streak in baseball history. Young is asked if it was nice to finally get the monkey off his back. "That wasn't a monkey," he says. "That was a zoo."

1 Before a game against the Marlins, Mets Manager Dallas Green explains to assembled reporters that he is sorry for the childish behavior of his players. Outfielder Vince Coleman has thrown an explosive at fans and pitcher Bret Saberhagen has sprayed bleach on reporters. It is a sincere, dramatic apology but it can't be heard because, for some reason, the theme song from *The Flintstones* is blaring from the speakers and being shown on the giant center-field scoreboard. Green is saying he will not tolerate silly behavior in his clubhouse and, as he says this, Fred is complaining to Wilma about having too much shampoo in his hair.

Top 5 Defensive Plays

5 There are two out in the bottom of the ninth inning and the Marlins are leading by a run. Atlanta's Otis Nixon, one of baseball's fastest men, is on third. Bryan Harvey throws a forkball in the dirt, and it bounces away from catcher Benito Santiago. Quick as a camera's flash, Santiago retrieves the ball and tags Nixon out at the plate to end the game. Lachemann says afterward that Santiago is the only catcher in the world who can make that play.

4 Marlins shortstop Walt Weiss preserves a Ryan Bowen shutout of Cincinnati by making a double play with runners on first and third. Weiss explains after the game that he can dunk a basketball, with two hands behind his head, and this explanation is necessary to describe the double play. Weiss got up as high as he could — on a ball Carr thought for sure was coming to him — and speared the line drive. "I guess," Bowen says, "some white men can jump."

3 In a game against San Diego, Santiago ends the game's largest threat by picking one of his old teammates off second base. He throws out Phil Plantier without ever leaving his knees.

2 Carr, running about as fast as a human can, makes his best catch of the year against the Cardinals. He dives, body fully extended about an inch off the ground, and his face skids across the artificial turf. He sticks his glove up, though, and the ball lands in the webbing. Right fielder Monty Fariss comes over to help Carr up. Did the cocky Carr say anything boastful? "He didn't have to," Fariss says. "He knew it was good."

1 Playing in Joe Robbie Stadium, right fielder Darrell Whitmore begins pursuit of a foul ball against the Phillies. He is a former college football player, which will soon come in handy. Whitmore runs about 50 yards and then, at full speed, runs into the bullpen wall. His legs flip completely over him and he does a handstand before falling on his back. He holds onto the ball. "That," Carr says, "was the catch of the season."

DARRELL TAKES A DIVE

Darrell Whitmore goes flying over the bullpen wall at full speed. He wound up doing a handstand before falling onto his back. Chuck Carr called it 'the catch of the season.' ESPN flipped over it too, repeatedly showing it on its highlight clips.

CARR FLIES...

TOP DEFENSIVE PLAYER

JOE RIMKUS JR.

ON A SCALE OF 10 . . .

Chuck Carr's leaping catch against Montreal would earn high marks from most judges, if not a trip to the trainer's room. 'I should be sponsored by Band-Aid,' Carr says.

...AND FLIES

A DAY AT THE RACES

Chuck Carr flashes some of the speed that helped him win the NL stolen-base title with 58. 'If I had Chuck's speed,' left fielder Jeff Conine said, 'I'd be hitting .900.'

C.M. GUERRERO

NOT THIS TIME

Carr was fast, but he wasn't perfect. This time he's tagged out at home by the Cubs' Rick Wilkins.

DAVID BERGMAN

A QUICK SNOOZE

Carr appears quite comfortable using second base as a pillow.

WALTER MICHOT

Top 5 Dramatic Victories

5 The Marlins rally forever, erasing five deficits against the Cubs. The 12-11 game ends, symbolically enough, with the pitcher ducking. Gary Sheffield hits a line drive right up the middle against Randy Myers to win the game in the bottom of the ninth.

4 Bob Natal, anonymous even when he isn't working behind his mask, hits a game-winning double in the bottom of the 15th inning. "It's nice to be the hero for a night," Natal says after the Marlins beat the Cubs, 3-2.

3 Rich Renteria, as if he's fighting for his family, singles to left field after fouling off seven pitches — two off

C.M. GUERRERO

CLOSE PLAY

Rich Renteria has a flair for dramatics, as third baseman Matt Williams and the Giants discovered.

his shin. The Marlins say it is the best at-bat of the season and, as a plus, it beats the Rockies in the bottom of the 12th inning, 7-6.

2 Marlins reliever Richie Lewis beats the Astros, 5-4, with his arm and his bat. Lewis gets the first hit of his major-league career, a single into the left-field corner to beat Houston in the bottom of the 13th inning. "It ranks right up there with getting married and having a baby," Lewis says.

1 It is special because it is the first. The Marlins beat the Dodgers, 6-3, on opening day. Charlie Hough is the winning pitcher and Bryan Harvey gets the save. Bret Barberie has the first hit in Marlins history, Walt Weiss the first RBI. One more thing: Hough and Marlins owner H. Wayne Huizenga had predicted victory.

Five Worst Losses

5 The Marlins lose to Atlanta, 4-3, the game decided without a pitch being thrown. Reliever Matt Turner, with Deion Sanders on third, is distracted. He changes his delivery in the middle of his motion and balks in the winning run. Turner says the umpires were just hot and wanted to leave. "Maybe," umpire Harry Wendelstedt says, "it was too hot for him."

4 The Marlins are leading first-place San Francisco, 6-2. But the Giants score three runs in the eighth and then, one strike away from a Marlins victory, Robby Thompson hits a two-strike pitch from Bryan Harvey into the left-field bleachers for a 7-6 victory. "I feel ill," Harvey says.

3 The Marlins are losing, 3-2, to San Francisco, but they load the bases with two out in the ninth. Orestes Destrade, Florida's mightiest man, is facing Rod Beck, one of baseball's best relievers. Destrade turns on a pitch and watches its flight. Right fielder Willie McGee has one thought: "This game is over." But the ball, hit about as hard as possible, hooks foul by less than five feet. Destrade's game-winning grand slam was but a long, loud strike. He goes on to strike out.

2 The Marlins lose, 13-5, to San Diego, after which Lachemann says the JRS fans "should ask for their money back." The Marlins are losing, 12-0, before they get their first hit. Benito Santiago is loudly booed, making two errors on one play and failing to get an out at the plate on three occasions when the Padres slide in safely. The crowd gives Santiago a loud, mocking cheer when he catches a simple popup.

1 The Marlins lose, 10-0, to the Pirates. The game's most symbolic play begins with Matias Carrillo grabbing a ball in right field and ends with Matias Carrillo grabbing it again at first base. The Marlins make four throws on the play, at least one to each base. Five players handle the ball. They get zero outs.

TOO LATE

Catcher Bob Natal waits for the throw, but the Cardinals' Todd Zeile makes it home safely.

C.M. GUERRERO

SEAN HAFFEY/SAN DIEGO UNION TRIBUNE

SOMETHING SMELLS ROTTEN

As part of the cost-cutting in San Diego, the Chicken has been replaced as mascot. Trying out for the role is one Genus Mephitis, aka Pepe LePew. Cynics might suggest Pepe would be a fine mascot, given the Padres' recent fortunes. We'll just say he managed to scare the Marlins more than the Chicken.

Top 5 Funniest Moments

5 In San Diego, Charlie Hough singles, breaking a small slump in which he is hitless for exactly 13 years. "If I hang that pitch to anybody else," San Diego pitcher Tim Scott says, "they might hit it out of the stadium." Hough has to borrow a bat because they no longer make bats with his signature. "You have to get a hit more than once every 13 years to have an autographed bat," Hough says.

4 Reliever Trevor Hoffman stops speaking to reporters because he has had a bad dream. In it, Hoffman hits a line drive that is clearly headed toward left field. Suddenly, just when he thinks he has a hit, a reporter sprints in from the right-field bullpen. The reporter is wearing an enormous glove. The reporter covers about 400 feet in two seconds and makes a perfect throw to complete the best play in baseball history. Hoffman's silence lasts an hour, until he starts telling reporters about his dream.

3 In Houston, reliever Matt Turner is suckered. Several teammates tell him that he is required to be at the ballpark by 4 p.m. Turner thinks he has missed the bus for a game after shopping too long for a pair of boots. The owner of the store drives him all the way to the Astrodome. Turner remembers, upon reaching the last highway exit, that the Marlins don't have a game that day.

2 During the fifth inning of a home game, Marlins owner H. Wayne Huizenga scampers onto the field with Billy The Marlin and does the hokey-pokey. Yes, he puts his backside in and puts his backside out and he shakes his $670 million backside all about. Huizenga didn't know how to do the hokeypokey, which is why he was spotted with Billy The Marlin an inning earlier, practicing by the batting cages under the stadium. His moves are so popular that, after each Florida home run, his hokey-pokey is flashed on the giant Joe Robbie Stadium scoreboard.

1 A crazed skunk runs on the field in San Diego, delaying the game for more than five minutes. San Diego reliever Pat Gomez throws a baseball at it, then says later he was hoping it would spray its fumes on Florida's shortstop and "kill him." The furry, foul creature scampers toward the Marlins' dugout, where the players trample each other to get out of its way. Orestes Destrade, saying skunks don't scare him because he has eaten potentially poisonous blowfish in Japan, is the only calm Marlin. He tries to feed the skunk sunflower seeds, but the skunk isn't hungry and runs underneath the stadium. Chuck Carr is by far the most scared, hitting his head on the dugout ceiling when one of the Marlins yells that the skunk has returned and then grabs Carr's ankle. "Don't those things bite?" pitcher Luis Aquino says. "They don't have skunks in Puerto Rico." Carr explains that he thought "skunks were only from Wisconsin."

FUNNY MOMENT HALL OF FAME NOMINEE

Teammates steal Chuck Carr's clothes during a game in Philadelphia. After his post game shower, a shivering Carr is left outside the locker room wearing a small white towel. The players have left creative replacement clothing for Carr and the other rookies. But Carr refuses to go to the airport wearing the only thing hanging in his locker, a very pretty blue tutu.

Carr demands his original clothes back, and is fined $500 for not playing along. He leaves the stadium angry.

First baseman Orestes Destrade, ever helpful, grabs the tutu and reminds Carr that he had forgotten it. Meanwhile, left fielder Jeff Conine scampers past autograph-seeking fans in a hot-pink blouse. Right fielder Darrell Whitmore does the same, except he's wearing a red dress.

ATTACK OF THE RUNAWAY TARP

The grounds crew (aided by ticket-office and concession workers) wrestles with the tarp during a rain delay. Manager Rene Lachemann had to rush out when one poor guy became trapped underneath. 'There were 22 blown rotator cuffs as they tried to pull the tarp on the field,' left fielder Jeff Conine said. 'It's the funniest thing I've ever seen.'

C.M. GUERRERO

ALL-STAR IMPORT
The Marlins lost three pitchers to get him, but third baseman Gary Sheffield gives Florida an All-Star who is only 24 years old.

DAVID BERGMAN

Top 5 Surprises

Three-way tie for fifth:

5 The Marlins, who had been thinking about building a domed stadium to combat the rain, suffer only one rainout all year.

5 Pitcher Chris Hammond hits two home runs — one more than starting shortstop Walt Weiss.

5 In his second appearance for the Marlins, Bryan Harvey gives up a home run and loses the game. Fans boo.

4 In their first season, the Marlins sweep both the Braves and the Pirates — the National League's two best teams a year earlier.

3 Everyone knew Bryan Harvey was good but not this good. He saves more games (45) than any National League reliever ever had before '93 and he does it for an expansion team. "Amazing," Harvey says.

2 Chuck Carr, only 25 but already given up on by four organizations, flourishes with the Marlins — leading the league in steals with 58.

1 The Marlins trade three pitchers — Trevor Hoffman, Jose Martinez and Andres Berumen — for one of the game's best players. Gary Sheffield, 24 years old, becomes the first expansion player to start in an All-Star Game and hits a home run in his first at-bat. The Houston Astros still don't have a player who has hit an All-Star home run.

5 After winning eight games in a row and being seriously considered for the All-Star team, pitcher Chris Hammond fails to break the record for victories by an expansion pitcher. Hammond needed only three victories in the season's last three months to tie. He got only one.

4 Gary Sheffield misses most of the season's final month because of an injured throwing shoulder. Partly because of his injury, Sheffield makes more errors (34) than any third baseman in baseball. One day after signing a four-year, $22.5 million contract, Sheffield makes three errors in one game.

3 The Marlins fail to reach one of their primary goals — to win 71 games, more than any previous expansion team.

2 Catcher Benito Santiago, a four-time All-Star, has the worst season of his career — offensively and defensively. He hits .230 and throws out just 23.7 percent of the runners trying to steal.

1 Right fielder Junior Felix, signed for $1.25 million a season, is so adventurous in the outfield that the Marlins release him halfway through the season.

Top 5 *Disappointments*

SANTIAGO STRUGGLES

Catcher Benito Santiago was a four-time All-Star who hit just .230. 'He can play a lot better,' General Manager Dave Dombrowski said.

WALTER MICHOT

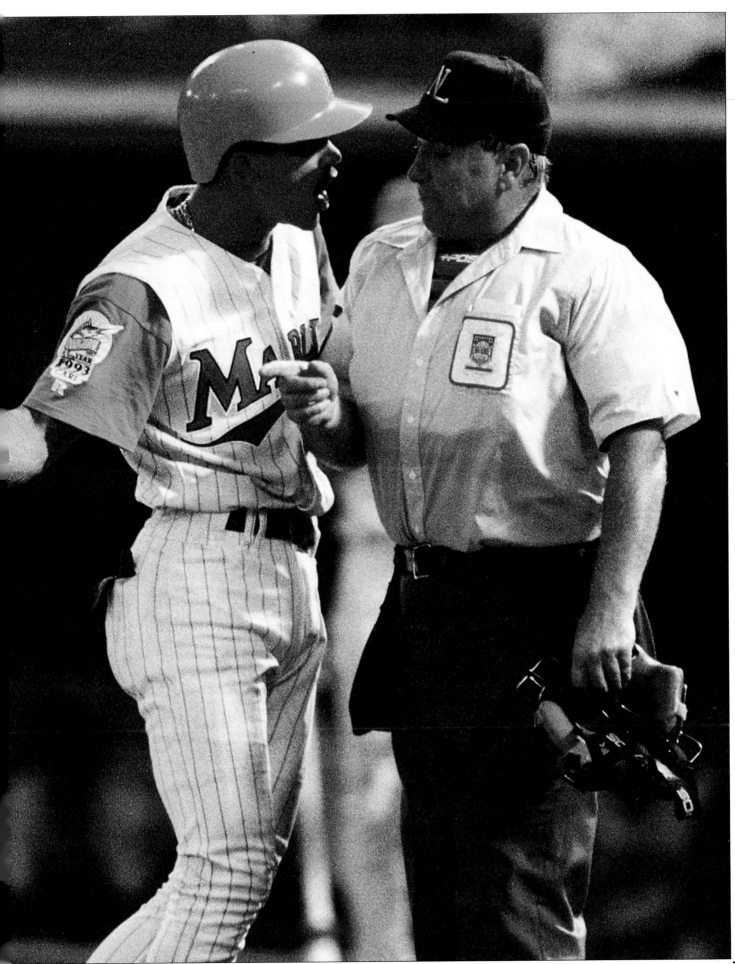

Top 5 Individual Performances

5 In a game against San Diego, leadoff man Chuck Carr has four hits and steals three bases. "If that guy gets on," says San Diego Tony Gwynn, "he could steal 100 to 120 bases a year, easily."

4 In a game against San Francisco, reserve outfielder Greg Briley hits two home runs. Briley, 5-8, hits one home run the rest of the season. "Sometimes I get myself in trouble because I think I'm 6-4," Briley says.

3 In a game against Pittsburgh, Gary Sheffield hits two home runs to continue his mastery of Bob Walk. Walk, in the past, has tried to get Sheffield out by throwing him a knuckleball and a blooper pitch. Sheffield has six hits off him, five of them homers.

2 Left fielder Jeff Conine goes four for four and steals a base. His achievement is all the more significant because he does it on the very first day of the season.

1 Cleanup man Orestes Destrade hits two home runs and knocks in six RBI in a 7-3 victory over first-place San Francisco. No Marlin has ever had so many RBI in one game. Later, against Chicago, Destrade hits two home runs in the same game again.

SAY IT IS SO, O

First baseman Orestes Destrade shows off a home-run swing that helped win over the hometown fans. After a slow start, he finished with a solid 20 home runs and 87 RBI.

JOE RIMKUS JR.

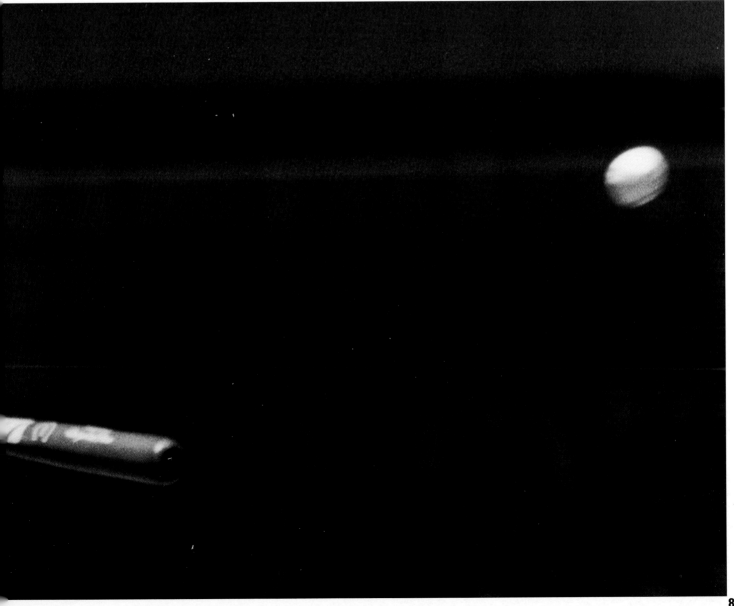

Top 5 fun facts we didn't have room for in the other categories

5 In spring training, infielder Alex Arias reveals that a troll doll named Paul brings him luck. "I get hits when I rub his orange hair," Arias explains. Gus Polidor, injured all spring, switches lockers because he thinks the doll is bringing him bad luck. Junior Felix sneaks a similar-looking doll in Polidor's locker, this one with blue hair and a guitar. Polidor is tormented. He doesn't switch lockers again, but the Marlins send him far, far away — to Triple A Edmonton in the minor leagues.

4 The Marlins rally dramatically, scoring seven runs in the seventh inning to take a lead on the Mets. But Bryan Harvey gives up a game-tying homer in the eighth inning, a two-run shot, and the Mets win in extra innings. They win when Jeromy Burnitz tags up and comes home. The Marlins appeal, saying Burnitz left third base early. The umpires disagree. Afterward, Burnitz admits he left early.

3 The Marlins sign outfielder Matias Carrillo, who has a tantalizing tale to tell. Carrillo is a former farmer who used to sleep outside on the ground and bathe in canals. Before going on a road trip, he needs the assistance of a sports writer to tie his tie. In his first two at-bats, Carrillo singles and doubles and drives in two runs.

2 Florida's new mascot is unveiled during spring training, landing near second base in a helicopter. Marlins General Manager Dave Dombrowski, in a moment of extraordinary goofiness, sprints out to hug his fat fish friend. Reliever Jim Corsi almost has his head severed by what he calls "that thing's beak" and wonders aloud how much trouble he would get into if he harpooned the team mascot.

1 In his first major-league start, 23-year-old David Weathers pitches perhaps the best game a Marlin ever has. He allows three hits and strikes out seven in a 2-0 victory over San Diego. Weathers is from Five Points, Tenn., a small town with no stoplights. "The population is 250," Weathers said, "if you count the pregnant people twice."

CHILLY ON BILLY

Billy faced a tough crowd when he was introduced as mascot. 'It looks like a mutant penguin,' left fielder Jeff Conine observed.

WALTER MICHOT

KNUCKLEBALL

Jeff Conine, left, and Chris Hammond give each other a knuck-le-high-five.

WALTER MICHOT

IN THE *WIN*

One of the real joys for Florida fans was following the season through the eyes and voices of radio broadcasters Joe Angel and Dave O'Brien. Although the two had never met before being hired by the Marlins, they fit together as well as ball and glove.

"I played in a celebrity golf tournament a month ago," O'Brien said in June, "and everybody told us they turn down the TV volume and listen to us. That kind of blows your mind. It's very gratifying."

When the Marlins won, Angel punctuated it by saying, "And this one is in the *WIN* column!" With Angel and O'Brien, even those in the loss column didn't seem so bad.

IN THE CHIN COLUMN

Dave O'Brien, left, and Joe Angel pack a punch on the air.

JOE RIMKUS JR.

COLUMN!

Angel: "By the way, Dave, as Ralph Kiner once said, 'On this Father's Day we want to wish all of you fathers a very happy birthday.' That's what he said. It's my birthday, and I had no idea. What did you get me?"

O'Brien: "A tie."

Angel: "After the way things have gone on this road trip, I feel like tying one on. So thank you for that. It will come in handy."

Angel: "We pause for station identification. This is the DAVE O'BRIEN Marlins radio network."

(Pause)

Angel: "It used to be MINE, but the kid is a comer. He's real aggressive."

O'Brien: "Joe, do you want to move those headphones?

"They're in my space."

Angel: "When my son Jonathan was born, I strongly considered naming him Iman. I'm glad I didn't. Could you imagine going through life, Iman Angel?"

O'Brien: "Yeah, those are the kinds of kids that grow up to be mass murderers with names like that."

Angel: "Boy, I'm glad I didn't do that. That would have killed me. Or *he* would have."

O'Brien: "And on that note, happy Father's Day, Joe."

DESTRADE

JOE RIMKUS JR.

ORESTES DESTRADE
FIRST BASE
.255, 20 HRS, 87 RBI

■ Had six RBI and two HRs Aug. 27 in 7-3 victory over first-place Giants.

■ After noticing that Ron Fraser's name was misspelled on a jersey during Ron Fraser Day, said, 'Hey, who are we honoring here? Walt Frazier? Smokin' Joe Frazier? Or that character from *Cheers*?'

■ Destrade, the day the Marlins took batting practice in shorts: 'I'm concerned about the guys with the real white legs. I don't want them to give us a bad image.'

SANTIAGO

BENITO SANTIAGO
CATCHER
.230, 13 HRS, 10 SB

■ Had homer and double in same inning against Astros.

■ Was fined $500 for oversleeping and being late to batting practice. Fine didn't put a dent in his wallet. That night in the same hotel suite he overslept in, he autographed baseballs for two hours. His fee: $10,000.

■ Cleveland catcher Junior Ortiz, on Santiago: 'He doesn't have an arm. He has a machete.'

WALTER MICHOT

BARBERIE

DAVID BERGMAN

BRET BARBERIE
SECOND BASE
.277, 16 2B, 33 RBI

■ Had 15-game hitting streak Aug. 7-22. Also went 14 of 19 games with at least two hits.

■ Spends the off-season disassembling and assembling cars. Owns a couple of 1950s Volkswagen vans and subscribes to a VW newsletter. 'I spent my whole off-season with my hands dirty, under a car,' Barberie said.

■ Barberie, on pickup baseball: 'I play in my apartment with some friends after midnight. We use half a bat and a rolled-up, taped-up sock. The neighbors are upset because we make noise. They've sent security over and put letters under my door.'

WALTER MICHOT

WALT WEISS
SHORTSTOP
.266, 79 BB

■ Despite saying he was so nervous that 'I felt like a rookie,' tripled in his first at-bat to drive in first two runs in Marlins history.

■ Wears No. 22 to honor childhood hero Mercury Morris, the former Dolphins running back. Weiss and Morris met for the first time during the season. Weiss said Morris was smaller than he thought. 'Yeah, I'm just an itty-bitty thing,' Morris said. 'But so is a bullet.'

■ Weiss, on the similarities between himself and Bret Barberie: 'We are about the same height. And both of us have kidneys.'

SHEFFIELD

DAVID BERGMAN

GARY SHEFFIELD
THIRD BASE
.294, 20 HRS, 73 RBI

■ Had two-HR game in 8-3 victory over Pirates and Bob Walk.

■ His uncle, Dwight Gooden, borrowed one of his bats and hit a home run against the Marlins. 'I told you not to use those bats until you left town,' Sheffield told him.

■ Sheffield, who had been sensitive to criticism in Milwaukee and San Diego, upon joining the Marlins: 'Before I break down, the whole stadium will have to fall down around me.'

WHITMORE

DAVID BERGMAN

DARRELL WHITMORE
RIGHT FIELD
.204, 8 2B, 3 E

■ Had a triple in first major-league at-bat during 3-1 victory over Expos.

■ For being a major leaguer, was given key to the city in his hometown of Front Royal, Va. He got it in the mail.

■ Whitmore, after his debut: 'What a welcome! I'm still shocked. Man, to get a triple in my first major-league at-bat . . . and a double, go two for four . . . '

CARR

CHUCK CARR
CENTER FIELD
.267, 19 2B, 58 SB

■ Had four hits, three stolen bases in 8-2 victory over Padres. After game, Tony Gwynn said if Carr got on base enough, he could steal '100 or 120 bases easily.'

■ When in Seattle organization, Carr once told teammate Ken Griffey Jr., 'I'm going to take your job.' Carr did start in center field for a couple of games but later was released.

■ Left stadium angry upon learning he won't start on opening day. Later said he'll laugh about this someday, 'when I'm in the Hall of Fame.'

DAVID BERGMAN

CONINE

JEFF CONINE
LEFT FIELD
.292, 24 2B, 79 RBI

■ Went four for four twice. Did it on opening day despite getting lost on the way to his new ballpark.

■ Conine and his bride, Cindy Doyaal, celebrated their honeymoon by playing in a racquetball doubles tournament.

■ After hitting a home run against Giants, described it as such: 'There are three inches on the bat, called the sweet spot. That pitch hit right in the middle of it, leaving 1 $\frac{1}{2}$ inches on each side of the sweet spot. I have played every sport you can imagine, but there is no better feeling in sports.'

DAVID BERGMAN

HAMMOND

WALTER MICHOT

CHRIS HAMMOND
PITCHER
11-12, 4.66 ERA, 108 KS

■ Won eight consecutive games and was NL pitcher of the month for June.

■ Went on his winning streak after changing his uniform number from 38 to 11.

■ Cincinnati General Manager Jim Bowden, after sending Hammond to Marlins for utility infielder Gary Scott and then watching Hammond blossom into a potential All-Star: 'It will probably go down in history as the worst trade I ever make.'

HOUGH

BILL FRAKES

CHARLIE HOUGH
PITCHER
9-16, 4.27 ERA, 126 KS

■ Shut out St. Louis for eight innings in 1-0 victory. 'That's the first time I've ever said, "Good, Bryan Harvey is coming in," ' Cardinals Manager Joe Torre said.

■ Been in baseball so long and knows so much about it that Los Angeles Dodgers call him for advice on trades, including the Eddie Murray deal.

■ Pittsburgh outfielder Andy Van Slyke, on facing Hough's knuckleball: 'It is like trying to hit while you're riding on a bike over railroad tracks.'

ARIAS

ALEX ARIAS
UTILITY
INFIELDER
.269, 20 RBI

■ Had home run in 2-0 victory over his former team, the Cubs, after saying he hadn't played in so long his bat felt heavy.

■ Once dated a girl but did not tell her what he did for a living because he was afraid she would be attracted to him merely because he plays baseball. Four months later she was wondering what job he could have that would include a four-month vacation and still be legal.

■ Arias, after beating the Cubs: 'It's special against them. Sometimes you just want to show them that you turned into a pretty decent player.'

JOE RIMKUS JR.

KLINK

BILL FRAKES

JOE KLINK
RELIEVER
0-2, 5.02 ERA, 22 KS

■ Graduate of Chaminade High in Hollywood dominated left-handers, holding them to a .216 average.

■ Klink, after the first spring-training game, surveyed a packed stadium and dozens of reporters: 'Last time I saw something like this? Just the World Series.'

BOWEN

RYAN BOWEN

JOE RIMKUS JR.

PITCHER

8-12, 4.42 ERA, 98 KS

■ Shut out St. Louis, 8-0, for first complete-game victory in Marlins history.

■ Won his first two starts after getting married during All-Star break. Manager Rene Lachemann went around suggesting all his pitchers hurry up and get married.

■ St. Louis Manager Joe Torre, after being beaten, 8-0, by Bowen: 'No way I can blame my hitters. When a guy throws that hard and is that wild it is hard to dig in on him.'

HARVEY

BRYAN HARVEY
RELIEVER
1.70 ERA, 45 SV, 73 KS

■ Had a streak of 21 appearances without allowing a run.

■ Was discovered while playing softball for a North Carolina team called Howard's Furniture.

■ Harvey, on what it felt like to be on All-Star team: 'This is awesome, just being around these guys. Gawwww-leeeee.'

ARMSTRONG

JOE RIMKUS JR.

JACK ARMSTRONG
PITCHER
9-17, 4.49 ERA, 118 KS

■ Gave up one run in seven innings in his next-to-last start, against the Cubs.

■ Armstrong lists his favorite book as *Zen & the Art of Motorcycle Maintenance*. It has nothing to do with the building of a motorcycle. It is a metaphoric look at how you can build your life the way a mechanic maintains his Harley. 'For example,' Armstrong said, eating from a bowl of fruit, 'right now, I'm changing my oil and I'm using the best oil you can buy.'

■ Armstrong, on why his former teammates didn't like him: 'I was arrogant to mask my insecurity. The dog barking loudest is always the most scared.'

RENTERIA

DAVID BERGMAN

RICH RENTERIA
UTILITY INFIELDER
.255, 9 2B, 30 RBI

■ Had three game-winning hits in season's first half and a squeeze bunt that won another. The squeeze was so good it brought home Chuck Carr from third even though Carr missed the sign.

■ Is exceedingly humble. Hours after beating Colorado with a 12th-inning hit in what Manager Rene Lachemann called the best pro at-bat he had ever seen, Renteria received a call from a friend. 'Did you play tonight?' his friend asked. 'Yeah, I got one hit,' Renteria replied, leaving it at that.

■ Renteria: 'I am a baseball player who lives paycheck to paycheck. I am a working man.'

1993 MARLINS RESULTS

APRIL   Home games are shaded

SUN	MON	TUES	WED	THURS	FRI	SAT
				1	2	3
4	**W** 5 6-3 LA	**L** 6 3-4 LA	**L** 7 2-4 LA	8	**L** 9 1-2 SD	**W** 10 2-1 SD
L 11 3-6 SD	**L** 12 3-4 (11) SF	**L** 13 1-3 SF	**W** 14 6-4 SF	15	**L** 16 3-9 HOU	**W** 17 9-4 HOU
L 18 0-3 HOU	19	**L** 20 4-5 ATL	**L** 21 4-7 ATL	**W** 22 4-3 ATL	**L** 23 4-5 COL	**W** 24 2-1 COL
W 25 11-1 COL	**L** 26 0-3 CIN	**W** 27 4-3 CIN	**W** 28 3-1 ATL	**W** 29 6-5 ATL	**L** 30 2-6 COL	

MAY

SUN	MON	TUES	WED	THURS	FRI	SAT
						W 1 7-6 (12) COL
L 2 1-2 COL	3	**W** 4 9-6 CIN	**L** 5 2-6 CIN	6	**L** 7 0-4 NY	**W** 8 4-2 NY
W 9 6-4 NY	**L** 10 0-1 NY	**L** 11 4-6 MTL	**W** 12 10-7 MTL	**L** 13 4-5 MTL	**L** 14 2-7 STL	**W** 15 8-0 STL
L 16 0-1 STL	**L** 17 3-10 PHI	**L** 18 0-6 PHI	**W** 19 5-3 PHI	20	**W** 21 5-3 CHI	**L** 22 1-2 CHI
23 **W** 4-2 CHI / 30 **L** 1-2 HOU	24	**L** 25 0-2 PIT	**W** 26 5-4 PIT	**L** 27 8-13 PIT	**W** 28 5-4 (12) HOU	**L** 29 2-4 HOU
	31					

JUNE

SUN	MON	TUES	WED	THURS	FRI	SAT
		1 1, **W** 7-3 SF 2, **L** 3-4	**L** 2 2-3 SF	3	**W** 4 6-2 SD	**W** 5 3-1 SD
W 6 9-2 SD	**W** 7 5-3 LA	**L** 8 1-2 LA	9	**W** 10 4-3 PIT	**W** 11 11-3 PIT	**W** 12 5-2 PIT
W 13 5-2 PIT	**L** 14 3-6 CHI	**L** 15 0-3 CHI	**L** 16 4-6 CHI	**W** 17 4-1 PHI	**L** 18 3-7 PHI	**L** 19 2-5 PHI
L 20 3-4 PHI	**L** 21 3-4 STL	**W** 22 7-5 STL	**L** 23 3-4 STL	24	**W** 25 3-1 MTL	**L** 26 2-4 MTL
W 27 9-2 MTL	28	**L** 29 9-10 (12) NY	**L** 30 1-7 NY			

MARLINS' FIRSTS

TEAM

- **Game:** April 5, vs. Los Angeles
- **Win:** April 5, 6-3 vs. Los Angeles
- **Loss:** April 6, 4-2 vs. Los Angeles
- **Road win:** April 14, 6-4 at San Francisco
- **Road loss:** April 12, 4-3 (11) at S.F.
- **Series win:** April 23-25, at Colorado (2-1)
- **Series sweep:** April 28-29, at Atl. (2-0)
- **Home series sweep:** June 10-13, Pittsburgh (4-0)
- **First winning road trip:** April 23-29, 5-2, at Colorado (2-1), at Cincinnati (1-1), at Atlanta (2-0)
- **Extra-inning game:** April 12, at San Francisco, 4-3 (11) loss
- **Extra-inning win:** May 1, vs. Colorado, 7-6 (12)
- **Complete game (for):** Ryan Bowen, May 10, 1-0 loss to New York
- **Complete game (against):** Armando Reynoso, April 30 vs. Colorado
- **Shutout (for):** Ryan Bowen, May 15 at Los Angeles
- **Shutout (against):** Pete Harnish and Doug Jones, four-hitter
- **Last at-bat win:** April 28, at Atlanta, 2 run top of ninth, 3-1 win
- **Come from behind win in ninth:** June 7, at Los Angeles, trailed, 3-2, won, 5-3
- **Multi-homer inning:** April 20, vs. Atlanta, Benito Santiago and Alex Arias off Greg Maddux, ninth inning
- **Ejection:** Doug Rader, May 8 at New York, third inning by Steve Rippley
- **Ejection (player):** Benito Santiago, June 18 at Philadelphia, fifth by Bruce Froemming
- **Time team leaves bench:** May 17 vs. Phila., after Alex Arias is hit by Dave West
- **Time team leaves bench due to animal visit**: June 5 at San Diego (Genus Mephitis) eighth inning
- **Rain delay (home):** May 19 vs. Philadelphia, start delayed seven minutes due to shower
- **Rainout (home):** May 31 vs. San Francisco
- **Double-header:** June 1 vs. San Francisco (split, 7-3, 3-4)

BATTERS

- **Batter:** Scott Pose, April 5 vs. L.A.
- **Base runner:** Scott Pose, vs. Los Angeles on April 5, first inning (E-4)
- **Hit:** Bret Barberie, vs. Los Angeles on April 5, first inning (single to center)
- **Run:** Benito Santiago, vs. Los Angeles on April 5
- **RBI:** Walt Weiss, vs. Los Angeles on April 5, second inning (two-run triple)

- **Extra-base hit:** Walt Weiss, vs. L.A on April 5, second inning (triple to right)
- **Double:** Orestes Destrade, vs. Los Angeles on April 5, third inning (left field)
- **Triple:** Walt Weiss, vs. Los Angeles on April 5, second inning off Orel Hershiser
- **Home run:** Benito Santiago, April 12 at San Francisco, sixth inning off Trevor Wilson (1-1 count)
- **Grand slam:** Junior Felix, April 25 at Colorado off Scott Aldred
- **Two homers in a game:** Greg Briley, June 1 vs. San Francisco off Bill Swift and Dave Burba (game one)
- **Home run to lead off a game:** Chuck Carr, June 1 vs. San Francisco off Bud Black
- **Home run in first major-league at-bat:** Mitch Lyden, June 16 at Chicago off Jose Bautista
- **Sacrifice:** Chris Hammond, April 7 vs. Los Angeles
- **Sacrifice fly:** Walt Weiss, April 17 at Houston off Darryl Kile (drove in Alex Arias)
- **Stolen base:** Jeff Conine, April 5 vs. Los Angeles, third base
- **Caught stealing:** Scott Pose, April 5 vs. Los Angeles, second base by Mike Piazza
- **Pinch hitter:** Alex Arias, April 5 vs. L.A.
- **Pinch hit:** Rich Renteria, April 14 at S.F.
- **Out:** Junior Felix, April 5 vs. Los Angeles by Hershiser (strikeout)
- **Base on balls:** Walt Weiss, April 5 vs. Los Angeles (Hershiser)
- **Hit by pitch:** Junior Felix, April 21 vs. Atlanta, by John Smoltz
- **Double play:** Bret Barberie, April 5 vs. Los Angeles second inning (line 7-3)
- **Grounded into double play:** Orestes Destrade, April 5 vs. Los Angeles (4-6-3)
- **Error:** Junior Felix, April 5 vs. Los Angeles (dropped fly)

PITCHING

- **Pitch:** Charlie Hough, vs. Los Angeles on April 5 at 2:12p.m. to Jose Offerman (called strike)
- **Strikeout:** Jose Offerman, April 5 vs. Los Angeles (by Hough, first inning, three pitches, swinging)
- **Strikeout the side:** Jack Armstrong, April 11 vs. San Diego (Gwynn, Gardner, Sheffield)
- **Walk allowed:** Eric Karros, April 5 vs. Los Angeles (by Hough)
- **Hit allowed:** Eric Davis, April 5 vs. Los Angeles (double to left off Hough)
- **Save:** Bryan Harvey, April 5 vs. Los Angeles
- **Home run allowed:** Tim Wallach, April 5 vs. Los Angeles (off Hough, sixth inning, solo, 2-2 count, 431 feet)
- **Run allowed:** Eric Karros, April 5 vs. Los Angeles (off Hough, driven in Jody Reed in fifth inning)
- **Unearned run:** Ryan Bowen, April 14 at San Francisco
- **Balk:** Richie Lewis, April 6 vs. Los Angeles

JULY

SUN	MON	TUES	WED	THURS	FRI	SAT
				W 1 7-5 NY	**W** 2 4-2 ATL	**L** 3 2-11 ATL
L 4 3-4 ATL	**L** 5 7-9 ATL	**L** 6 3-8 COL	**L** 7 5-6 COL	**L** 8 2-3 COL	**L** 9 1-5 ATL	**W** 10 5-2 ATL
L 11 3-6 ATL	12 ALL-STAR BREAK	13	14	**L** 15 4-7 CIN	**L** 16 0-4 CIN	**W** 17 6-3 CIN
L 18 3-5 CIN	**W** 19 3-1 COL	**L** 20 3-6 COL	**W** 21 6-4 COL	**L** 22 3-7 CIN	**L** 23 2-3 CIN	**W** 24 2-0 CIN
W 25 7-3 CIN	26	**L** 27 3-4 NY	**L** 28 4-5 NY	**W** 29 2-1 NY	**L** 30 1-11 MTL	**L** 31 5-6 MTL

AUGUST

SUN	MON	TUES	WED	THURS	FRI	SAT
W 1 5-4 MTL	**L** 2 3-5 STL	**W** 3 1-0 STL	**L** 4 2-10 STL	**L** 5 6-16 STL	**W** 6 4-3 PHI	**L** 7 7-8 (10) PHI
W 8 6-5 PHI	**W** 9 3-2 CHI	**W** 10 3-2 (15) CHI	**W** 11 12-11 CHI	**L** 12 1-5 CHI	**L** 13 3-6 PIT	**W** 14 8-3 PIT
L 15 3-4 (11) PIT	16	**L** 17 0-4 HOU	**L** 18 1-2 HOU	**L** 19 3-8 HOU	**W** 20 5-4 SF	**L** 21 4-7 SF
L 22 6-7 SF	23	**L** 24 0-4 HOU	**L** 25 2-3 HOU	**W** 26 5-4 (13) HOU	**W** 27 7-4 SF	28
L 29 3-9 SF	**L** 30 1-5 SF	**W** 31 2-1 SD				

SEPTEMBER

SUN	MON	TUES	WED	THURS	FRI	SAT
			L 1 5-13 SD	**W** 2 6-1 SD	**L** 3 4-5 (13) LA	**L** 4 4-9 LA
W 5 4-3 LA	**W** 6 2-0 SD	**L** 7 4-6 SD	**L** 8 2-3 SD	**L** 9 5-6 (10) LA	**W** 10 2-1 LA	**W** 11 3-2 LA
L 12 0-1 LA	13	**L** 14 0-1 PIT	**L** 15 1-8 PIT	**L** 16 0-10 PIT	**W** 17 2-0 CHI	**L** 18 5-6 CHI
W 19 2-1 CHI	**L** 20 1-7 PHI	**L** 21 3-5 PHI	**L** 22 1-2 (12) PHI	23	**L** 24 5-9 STL	**W** 25 2-1 STL
L 26 7-10 STL	**W** 27 3-1 MTL	**L** 28 2-3 MTL	**L** 29 1-7 MTL	**L** 30 3-5 MTL		

OCTOBER

SUN	MON	TUES	WED	THURS	FRI	SAT
					L 1 1-4 NY	**L** 2 1-7 NY
L 3 2-9 NY	4	5	6	7	8	9

C.M. GUERRERO

OOPS

Gary Sheffield made 34 errors this season, most among third basemen in the National League. Still, Sheffield refused to get distraught. 'When it all clicks, I'm going to be one of the best in the game,' he said.

HIGHS & LOWS

GENERAL

Most consecutive wins: 4, twice (last: Aug. 8-11)

Most consecutive losses: 7, July 3-9

Highest attendance, home: 45,796, Aug. 27 vs. San Francisco

Highest attendance, road: 71,192, April 25 vs. Colorado

Lowest attendance, home: 24,064, Sept. 2 vs. San Diego

Lowest attendance, road: 7,092, Sept. 7 vs. San Diego

Longest game, time: 4:51, Sept. 4 vs. Los Angeles (L, 5-4 in 13 innings)

Longest game, 9 innings: 3:63, Aug. 11 vs. Chicago (W, 12-11)

Shortest game, time: 1:41, Sept. 14 vs. Pittsburgh (L, 1-0 in 6 innings)

Shortest game, time (9 innings): 2:09, May 26 vs. Pittsburgh

Longest game, innings: 15, Aug. 10 vs. Chicago (W, 3-2)

Largest winning margin: 10, 11-1; Apr. 25 vs. Colorado

Largest losing margin: 10, twice (last: Aug. 5 vs. St. Louis, 16-6)

Best homestand (by pct.): 1,000, June 10-13 (4-0)

Worst homestand (by pct.): .000, Sept. 14-16 vs. Pittsburgh

Best road trip (by pct.): .800, 4-1; June 4-8

Worst road trip (by pct.): .143, 1-6; twice (last: July 2-8)

Most runners left on base, game: 17; twice (last: Aug. 26 vs. Houston)

Most errors, game: 4, twice (last: Sept. 30 vs. Montreal)

Most double plays, game: 3, (last: Sept. 3 vs. Los Angeles)

TEAM BATTING

Most runs, game: 12, Aug. 10 vs. Chicago

Most runs, inning: 8, April 25 vs. Colorado (fourth)

Most hits, game: 21, June 11 vs. Pittsburgh

Most hits, inning: 8, April 26 vs. Colorado (fourth)

Fewest hits, game: 3, 5 times (last: Sept. 16 vs. Pittsburgh)

Most doubles, game: 5, twice (last: July 1 vs. New York)

Most triples, game: 3, June 17 vs. Philadelphia

Most home runs, game: 3 times (last: Aug. 22 vs. San Francisco)

Most home runs, inning: 2, 3 times (last: Aug. 8 vs. Philadelphia)

Most consecutive games, homer: 6, twice (last: Aug. 27-Sept 3)

Most consecutive games, no homer: 6,

Sept. 25-Oct. 3

Most extra-base hits, game: 7, June 11 vs. Pittsburgh (5 2B, 1 3B, 1 HR)
Most walks, game: 11, 3 times (last: Aug. 28 vs. Houston)
Fewest walks, game: 0, 12 times (last: Aug. 21 vs. San Francisco
Most strikeouts, game: 13, 3 times (last: July 4 vs. Atlanta)
Fewest strikeouts, game: 1, twice (last: April 28 vs. Atlanta)
Most stolen bases, game: 6, April 29 vs. Atlanta)

TEAM PITCHING

Fewest runs, game: 0, 5 times (last: Sept. 17 vs. Chicago)
Most runs, game: 16, Aug. 5 vs. St. Louis
Fewest hits, game: 3, 7 times (last: Sept. 25 vs. St. Louis)
Most hits, game: 19, twice (last: Sept. 16 vs. Pittsburgh)
Most home runs, game: 4, twice (last: July 15 vs. Atlanta)
Most walks, game: 12, Aug. 17 vs. Philadelphia
Fewest walks, game: 0, 9 times (last: Aug. 31 vs. San Diego)
Most strikeouts, game: 13, twice (last: Sept. 3 vs. Los Angeles)
Most consecutive strikeouts: 6, June 21 vs St. Louis

INDIVIDUAL BATTING

Most at-bats, game: 7, 5 times (last: Carr, Sept. 3 vs. Los Angeles)
Most runs, game: 3, 7 times (last: Barberie, Sept. 2 vs. San Diego)
Most hits, game: 4, 11 times (last: Renteria, Sept. 3 vs. Los Angeles)
Most doubles, game: 2, 12 times (last: Barberie, Sept. 7 vs. San Diego)
Most triples, game: 1, 30 times (last: Sheffield, Sept. 7 vs. San Diego)
Most home runs, game: 2, 4 times (last: Destrade, Sept. 18 vs. Chicago)
Most extra-base hits, game: 2, 34 times (last: Destrade, Sept. 18 Chicago)
Most total bases, game: 9, twice (last: Destrade, Aug. 27 vs. San Francisco)
Most RBI, game: 6, Destrade, Aug. 27 vs. San Francisco
Most sac flies, game: 2, Sheffield, Aug. 21 vs. San Francisco
Most hit by pitch, game: 2, Barberie, Aug. 27 vs. San Francisco)
Most walks, game: 4, Weiss, Aug. 26 vs. Houston
Most strikeouts, game: 4, Destrade, July 5 vs. Atlanta
Most stolen bases, game: 3, 3 times (last: Carr, Sept. 2 vs. San Diego)
Longest hitting streak: 15, twice (Barberie, Aug. 7-22)

INDIVIDUAL PITCHING

Longest winning streak: 8, Hammond (May 26-July 15)
Longest losing streak: 7, Hammond (July 15 to Sept. 14)
Most inning pitched, starter: 9.0, twice (last: Sept. 2 vs San Diego)
Most innings pitched, reliever: 3.0, 10 times (last: Lewis, Sept. 14 vs. Pittsburgh)

ROSTER

PITCHERS

No.	Name	B-T	Ht.	Wt.	Born	Birthplace	'92 club
27	Luis Aquino	R-R	6-1	190	5-19-65	Santurce, Puerto Rico	Kansas City
77	Jack Armstrong	R-R	6-5	220	3-7-65	Englewood, N.J.	Cleveland
46	Ryan Bowen	R-R	6-0	185	2-10-68	Hanford, Calif.	Houston
44	Cris Carpenter*	R-R	6-1	185	4-5-65	St. Augustine, Fla.	St. Louis
41	Jim Corsi	R-R	6-1	220	9-9-61	Newton, Mass.	Oakland
11	Chris Hammond	L-L	6-1	195	1-21-66	Atlanta	Cincinnati
34	Bryan Harvey	R-R	6-2	212	6-2-63	Chattanooga, Tenn.	California
51	Trevor Hoffman*	R-R	6-1	200	10-13-67	Bellflower, Calif.	Nashville
49	Charlie Hough	R-R	6-2	190	1-5-48	Honolulu	Chi. (AL)
40	John Johnstone	R-R	6-3	195	11-25-68	Liverpool, N.Y.	Binghamton
58	Joe Klink	R-L	5-11	175	2-3-62	Johnstown, Pa.	Oakland
24	Richie Lewis	R-R	5-6	175	1-25-66	Muncie, Ill.	Baltimore
57	Bob McClure*	S-L	5-11	188	4-29-53	Oakland	St. Louis
31	Robb Nen	R-R	6-4	200	11-28-69	San Pedro, Calif.	Tulsa
48	Pat Rapp	R-R	6-3	205	7-13-67	Jennings, La.	San Fran.
42	Rich Rodriguez	R-L	6-0	200	3-1-63	Downey, Calif.	San Diego
54	Matt Turner	R-R	6-5	215	2-18-67	Lexington, Ky.	Tucson
35	David Weathers	R-R	6-3	205	9-25-69	Five Points, Tenn.	Toronto

CATCHERS

No.	Name	B-T	Ht.	Wt.	Born	Birthplace	'92 club
55	Steve Decker	R-R	6-3	220	10-25-65	Rock Island, N.Y.	San Fran.
52	Mitch Lyden	R-R	6-3	225	12-44-64	Portland, Ore.	Tidewater
50	Terry McGriff	R-R	6-2	195	9-23-63	Fort Pierce, Fla.	Syracuse
13	Bob Natal	R-R	5-11	190	11-13-65	Long Beach, Calif.	Montreal
09	Benito Santiago	R-R	6-1	185	3-9-65	Ponce, Puerto Rico	San Diego

INFIELDERS

No.	Name	B-T	Ht.	Wt.	Born	Birthplace	'92 club
26	Alex Arias	R-R	6-9	185	11-20-67	New York	Chi. (NL)
8	Bret Barberie	S-R	5-11	180	8-16-67	Long Beach, Calif.	Montreal
39	Orestes Destrade	S-R	6-5	230	5-8-62	Santiago, Cuba	Japan
18	Dave Magadan*	L-R	6-3	205	9-30-62	Tampa	N.Y. (NL)
14	Gus Polidor	R-R	6-0	180	10-26-61	Caracas, Venezuela	Tacoma
6	Rich Renteria	R-R	5-9	175	12-25-61	Harbor City, Calif.	Jalisco
10	Gary Sheffield	R-R	5-11	190	11-18-68	Tampa	San Diego
22	Walt Weiss	S-R	6-0	175	11-28-63	Tuxedo, N.Y.	Oakland

OUTFIELDERS

No.	Name	B-T	Ht.	Wt.	Born	Birthplace	'92 club
16	Geronimo Berroa*	R-R	6-0	195	3-18-65	Santo Domingo, D.R.	Cincinnati
20	Greg Briley*	L-R	5-8	180	5-24-65	Greenville, N.C.	Seattle
21	Chuck Carr	S-R	5-10	165	9-10-65	S. Bernandino, Calif.	St. Louis
25	Matias Carrillo	L-L	5-11	190	2-24-63	Los Mochis, Mexico	Mexico City
19	Jeff Conine	R-R	6-1	220	6-27-66	Tacoma, Wash.	Kansas City
29	Henry Cotto	R-R	6-2	180	1-5-61	Bronx, N.Y.	Seattle
3	Carl Everett	S-R	6-0	181	6-3-70	Tampa	P. William
4	Monty Fariss*	R-R	6-4	205	10-13-67	Cordell, Okla.	Texas
47	Junior Felix*	S-R	5-11	165	10-3-67	Laguna Salada, DR	California
2	Scott Pose	L-R	5-11	165	2-11-67	Davenport, Iowa	Chattan'ga
17	Darrell Whitmore	L-R	6-1	210	11-18-68	Front Royal, Va.	Kinston
30	Nigel Wilson	L-L	6-1	185	1-12-70	Oshawa, Ontario	Knoxville

* Traded or released.

Manager: Rene Lachemann (15)
Coaches: Marcel Lachemann (53), Vada Pinson (28), Doug Rader (12), Frank Reberger (33), Cookie Rojas (1)

Fewest hits, complete game: 3, Twice (last: Hammond, Sept. 14 vs. Pittsburgh)
Fewest walks, complete game: 1, Hammond, Sept. 15 vs. Pittsburgh
Most walks, game: 7, 3 times (last: Armstrong, Aug. 7 vs. Philadelphia)
Most strikeouts, game: 10, Armstrong (April 11 vs. San Diego)
Most strikeouts in relief: 6, Turner, June 2 vs. San Francisco (2.2 IP)
Most strikeouts, inning: 3, 15 times (last:

Turner, Sept. 28 vs. Montreal, ninth)
Most consecutive strikeouts: 5, Armstrong (April 11 San Diego)
Most home runs allowed, game: 3, 4 times (last: Armstrong, Aug. 12 vs. Chicago)
Most consecutive scoreless innings (starter): 17, Bowden (May 10-21)
Most consecutive scoreless innings (relief): 18.1, Harvey (May 9-June 22)

CEREMONIAL FIRST PITCH
Joe DiMaggio — Carl Barger's favorite player — does the honors on opening day.

JOE RIMKUS JR.

DAVID BERGMAN

THAT'S GRATITUDE
It's only a sign on a bedsheet, but it sums up a community's feelings.

1993 STATISTICS

BATTING

Players	Avg.	OBA	AB	R	H	2B	3B	HR	RBI	BB	SO	SF	HBP	SB-CS	E
Mitch Lyden	.300	.300	10	2	3	0	0	1	1	0	3	0	0	0-0	0
Henry Cotto	.296	.312	135	15	40	7	0	3	14	3	18	1	1	11-1	2
Gary Sheffield**	.294	.361	494	67	145	20	5	20	73	47	64	7	9	17-5	34
Sheffield (Fla.)	.292	.378	236	33	69	8	3	10	37	29	34	4	6	12-4	19
Jeff Conine	.292	.351	595	75	174	24	3	12	79	52	135	5	5	2-2	2
Dave Magadan*	.286	.400	227	22	65	12	0	4	29	44	30	3	1	0-1	7
Bret Barberie	.277	.344	375	45	104	16	2	5	33	33	58	3	6	2-4	9
Alex Arias	.269	.344	249	27	67	5	1	2	20	27	18	3	3	1-1	6
Chuck Carr	.267	.327	551	75	147	19	2	4	41	49	74	4	2	58-22	6
Walt Weiss	.266	.367	500	50	133	14	2	1	39	79	73	4	3	7-3	15
Matias Carrillo	.255	.281	55	4	14	6	0	0	3	1	7	0	1	0-0	0
O. Destrade	.255	.324	569	61	145	20	3	20	87	58	130	6	3	0-2	19
Rich Renteria	.255	.314	263	27	67	9	2	2	30	21	31	1	2	0-2	2
Junior Felix*	.238	.267	214	25	51	11	1	7	22	10	50	0	1	2-1	6
Benito Santiago	.230	.291	469	49	108	19	6	13	50	37	88	4	5	10-7	11
Bob Natal	.214	.273	117	3	25	4	1	1	6	6	22	1	4	1-0	0
Darrell Whitmore	.204	.249	250	24	51	8	2	4	19	10	72	0	5	4-2	3
Scott Pose	.195	.233	41	0	8	2	0	0	3	2	4	0	0	0-2	0
Greg Briley*	.194	.250	170	17	33	6	0	3	12	12	42	1	1	6-2	1
Monty Fariss*	.172	.294	29	3	5	2	1	0	2	5	13	0	0	0-0	0
Gus Polidor	.167	.167	6	0	1	1	0	0	0	0	2	0	0	0-0	0
G. Berroa*	.118	.167	34	3	4	1	0	0	1	2	7	0	0	0-0	0
Carl Everett	.105	.150	19	0	2	0	0	0	0	1	9	0	0	1-0	1
Terry McGriff	.000	.200	7	0	0	0	0	0	0	1	2	0	0	0-0	0
Steve Decker	.000	.158	15	0	0	0	0	0	1	3	3	1	0	0-0	1
Nigel Wilson	.000	.000	16	0	0	0	0	0	0	0	11	0	0	0-0	0
Totals	**.248**	**.314**	**5475**	**581**	**1356**	**197**	**31**	**94**	**542**	**498**	**1054**	**43**	**51**	**117-56**	**125**

Sacrifice bunts: Carr 7, Barberie 5, Weiss 5, Natal 3, Renteria 3, Whitmore 2, Arias, Briley, Carrillo, Cotto, Destrade.

PITCHING

Pitching	W-L	ERA	G-GS	Sv	IP	H	R	ER	HR	BB	K
Bryan Harvey (R)	1-5	1.70	59-0	45	69.0	45	14	13	4	13	73
Cris Carpenter* (R)	0-1	2.89	29-0	0	37.1	29	15	12	1	15	26
Matt Turner (R)	4-5	2.91	55-0	0	68.0	55	23	22	7	26	59
Richie Lewis (R)	6-3	3.26	57-0	0	77.1	68	37	28	7	43	65
T. Hoffman* (R)	2-2	3.28	28-0	2	35.1	24	13	13	5	19	26
Luis Aquino (R)	6-8	3.42	38-13	0	110.2	115	43	42	6	40	67
R. Rodriguez (L)**	2-4	3.79	70-0	3	76.0	73	38	32	10	33	43
Rodriguez (Florida)	0-1	4.11	36-0	1	46.0	39	23	21	8	24	21
Pat Rapp (R)	4-6	4.02	16-16	0	94.0	101	49	42	7	39	57
Charlie Hough (R)	9-16	4.27	34-34	0	204.1	202	109	97	20	71	126
Ryan Bowen (R)	8-12	4.42	27-27	0	156.2	156	83	77	11	87	98
Jack Armstrong (R)	9-17	4.49	36-33	0	196.1	210	105	98	29	78	118
Chris Hammond (L)	11-12	4.66	32-32	0	191.0	207	106	99	18	66	108
Joe Klink (L)	0-2	5.02	59-0	0	37.2	37	22	21	0	24	22
Dave Weathers (R)	2-3	5.12	14-6	0	45.2	57	26	26	3	13	34
John Johnstone (R)	0-2	5.91	7-0	0	10.2	16	8	7	1	7	5
Jim Corsi (R)	0-2	6.64	15-0	0	20.1	28	15	15	1	10	7
Robb Nen (R)	1-0	7.02	15-1	0	33.1	35	28	26	5	20	27
Bob McClure* (L)	1-1	7.11	14-0	0	6.1	13	5	5	2	5	6
Totals	**64-98**	**4.13**	**162-162**	**48**	**1440.1**	**1437**	**724**	**661**	**135**	**598**	**945**

* Traded or released; ** Combined San Diego and Florida statistics.

FIRST BOXSCORE

MARLINS 6, DODGERS 3

Los Angeles	ab	r	h	bi	bb	so	av.
Jose Offerman ss	4	0	1	1	1	2	.250
Brett Butler cf	4	0	0	0	0	2	.000
Darryl Strawberry rf	3	0	0	0	1	0	.000
Eric Davis lf	4	0	1	0	0	1	.250
Tim Wallach 3b	4	1	1	1	0	1	.250
Eric Karros 1b	3	1	1	0	1	0	.333
Mike Piazza c	4	0	1	0	0	0	.250
Jody Reed 2b	4	1	2	1	0	1	.500
Orel Hershiser p	2	0	1	0	0	0	.500
Roger McDowell p	0	0	0	0	0	0	.—
Lenny Harris, ph	1	0	0	0	0	0	.000
Cory Snyder ph	1	0	0	0	0	0	.000
Rick Trlicek p	0	0	0	0	0	0	.—
Dave Hansen ph	1	0	0	0	0	0	.000
Totals	**34**	**3**	**8**	**3**	**3**	**7**	

Florida	ab	r	h	bi	bb	so	av.
Scott Pose cf-lf	5	0	1	2	0	0	.200
Bret Barberie 2b	4	1	2	0	0	1	.500
Junior Felix rf	4	0	1	0	0	1	.250
Cris Carpenter p	0	0	0	0	0	0	.—
Orestes Destrade 1b	4	1	1	0	0	1	.250
Bryan Harvey p	0	0	0	0	0	0	.—
Dave Magadan 3b	4	1	2	0	0	0	.500
Benito Santiago c	4	1	2	1	0	0	1.000
Jeff Conine lf-1b	4	2	4	0	0	1	.667
Walt Weiss ss	3	1	2	2	1	0	.667
Charlie Hough p	2	0	0	0	0	1	.000
Alex Arias ph	1	0	0	0	0	0	.000
Luis Aquino p	0	0	0	0	0	0	.—
Joe Klink p	0	0	0	0	0	0	.—
Chuck Carr cf	1	0	0	0	0	1	.000
Totals	**36**	**6**	**14**	**5**	**1**	**3**	

Los Angeles	000 021 000—3	8	2
Florida	031 001 10x—6	14	1

E—Wallach (1); Reed (1), Felix (1). LOB—Los Angeles 7, Florida 4. 2B—E.Davis (1), Karros (1), Destrade (1). 3B—Weiss (1). HR—Wallach (1) off Hough. RBI—Offerman (1), Wallach (1), Reed (1), Pose 2 (2), Santiago (1), Weiss 2 (2). SB—Conine (1). CS—Pose (1). GIDP—.Piazza, Destrade.
Runners left in scoring position—Los Angeles 3 (Strawberry, Karros, Piazza); Florida 4 (Pose, Magadan, Hough 2). GIDP—Piazza, Destrade.
Runners left in scoring position—Los Angeles 3 (Strawberry, Karros, Piazza); Florida 4 (Pose, Magadan, Hough 2).
Runners moved up—Davis, Piazza, Pose, Magadan, Weiss.
DP—Los Angeles 2 (E.Davis and Karros), (Reed, Offerman and Karros); Florida 1 (Magadan, Barberie and Destrade).

Los Angeles	ip	h	r	er	bb	so	np	era
O. Hershiser L, 0-1	5	10	5	5	1	3	64	9.00
Roger McDowell	1	0	0	0	0	0	8	0.00
Rick Trlicek	2	4	1	0	0	0	24	4.50

Florida	ip	h	r	er	bb	so	np	era
C. Hough W, 1-0	6	6	3	3	2	4	96	4.50
Luis Aquino	0	1	0	0	0	0	2	0.00
Joe Klink	1	0	0	0	1	1	13	0.00
Cris Carpenter	1	0	0	0	0	1	17	0.00
Bryan Harvey S, 1	1	1	0	0	0	1	20	0.00

Hershiser pitched to 2 batters in the 6th, Aquino pitched to 1 batter in the 7th, Klink pitched to 1 batter in the 8th.
Inherited runners-scored—McDowell 2-1, Carpenter 1-0, Klink 1-0.
T—2:43. A—42,334.

PICTURES
Herald's Marlins Photographers

C.M. GUERRERO	WALTER MICHOT	JOE RIMKUS JR.	DAVID BERGMAN
BOTTOM LEFT	TOP LEFT	BOTTOM RIGHT	TOP RIGHT
EL NUEVO HERALD	THE MIAMI HERALD	THE MIAMI HERALD	THE MIAMI HERALD

GRAPHICS ARTWORK
Derek Hembd

PRODUCTION COORDINATION
Cathy Kirkland

WORDS

Unforgettable, from start to finish

Baseball is all about things you hold onto. The ball, the bat and the glove. The autograph, the baseball card and the pennant. The peanuts, the popcorn and the Cracker Jacks. The game has those moments, too, when it makes you hold your breath.

But those aren't the things I'll hold onto from 1993, the year the Marlins waddled from the womb. No, I refuse to clutch anything that can be acquired easily, at any old ballpark with artificial turf and no view of heaven.

So you won't find my keepsake in a stadium souvenir stand, won't find it in any book that lists the worth of DiMaggio's autograph or Clemente's rookie card. My treasure will be worth more years from now and it will never get lost, not after I give it to my first son.

It will never slip through his fingers.

You don't hold memories in your hand.

I'll remember Charlie Hough making everyone laugh. I'll remember Dave Magadan about to cry.

I'll remember Rene Lachemann's smile as he blew kisses to the crowd. I'll remember Rene Lachemann's chin dropping after losing on the last pitch.

I'll remember Ryan Bowen pitching poetically. I'll remember Ryan Bowen usually having one inning that didn't rhyme with the rest.

I'll remember Walt Weiss hitting one home run. I'll remember Chris Hammond hitting two.

I'll remember Bret Barberie enjoying the game so much he played it in his apartment, with a taped-up sock instead of a baseball. I'll remember an injured Bret Barberie hurting so much that he didn't even watch the games on TV.

I'll remember Rich Renteria being a miracle dressed as a Marlin. I'll remember Greg Briley being a strikeout dressed as one.

I'll remember Charlie Hough's floatball. I'll remember Robb Nen's fastball.

I'll remember Walt Weiss being solid and steady. I'll remember Junior Felix being everything but.

I'll remember Orestes Destrade hitting a home run and the crowd asking him out of the dugout. I'll remember Orestes Destrade striking out and the crowd asking him out of the lineup.

I'll remember Chuck Carr making a catch in St. Louis that no one else makes. I'll remember Chuck Carr dropping a ball in Los Angeles that no one else drops.

I'll remember Gary Sheffield's nuclear swing. I'll remember Gary Sheffield's radioactive glove.

I'll remember Benito Santiago's million-dollar arm. I'll remember Benito Santiago's millionaire attitude.

I'll remember Chris Hammond being so good. I'll remember Chris Hammond being so bad.

I'll remember Jack Armstrong thinking like a pitcher. I'll remember Jack Armstrong pitching like a thinker.

I'll remember Matt Turner succeeding after six years of failure. I'll remember Bob McClure failing after 16 years of success.

I'll remember how happy Trevor Hoffman was to come to the Marlins. I'll remember how sad Trevor Hoffman was to leave them.

I'll remember the season starting with sun, triumph and Jeff Conine being as perfect as the afternoon. I'll remember the season ending with rain, defeat and a home run by a New York Met who had been fired before the game.

I'll remember.

DAN LE BATARD
The Miami Herald

DAN LE BATARD
Height, weight: 6-4, 200.
Bats: Right. **Throws:** Right.
Writes: Right.
Drafted: Out of the University of Miami.
Acquired: Free agent. **Born:** 12/16/68 in Jersey City, N.J. **Home:** Miramar, Fla.
Professional: Just completed rookie season as Marlins beat reporter for The Miami Herald, although major-league baseball experience includes having covered the past three World Series. . . . Previously covered University of Miami football and baseball.
Personal: Mom says was always writing stories in crayon, a practice he continues to this day. . . . Father foresook putting baseball in crib, went with keyboard. . . . Hobbies include basketball, reading. . . . Attended Hollywood Chaminade High and graduated from UM with degrees in journalism and politics. . . . Knew had to change athletic pursuits when most at-bats ended with creative adjectives.

LAST OUT!

DAVID BERGMAN

CAPPING IT OFF
Manager Rene Lachemann takes his hat off to the fans at JRS as the inaugural season becomes a memory.